Yorkshire Terriers

Sharon L. Vanderlip, DVM

BARRON'S

Contents

Yorkshire Terrier History

The Yorkshire Terrier is the most popular terrier breed in the world—and the sixth-most popular dog breed in the United States. And it's no wonder. This toy terrier with the flowing, silky coat, alluring countenance, and portable size is beautiful, bright, and bonds closely with its owner.

YORKIE ANCESTORS

The Yorkie shares its ancient ancestry with all dog breeds, tracing back to a creature that looked like a cross between a weasel and a fox, called Hesperocyonines. This primitive animal evolved in North America about 40 million years ago. Hesperocyonines gave rise to many canine species before it became extinct 15 million years ago.

Over the several million years that followed, prehistoric canids eventually developed into the first wild dogs. The Yorkie's diminutive size and endearing expression belie the fact that, like all members of the domestic dog species (known as *Canis familiaris*), the Yorkshire Terrier is a direct descendant of the gray wolf and shares 98.2 percent of its genetic material in common with this very close wild ancestor.

Dogs were the first animals to be domesticated by humans, although precisely when and where remain topics of lively debate. Archaeologists contend that the fossil evidence places canine evolution somewhere between 13,000 and 20,000 years ago, most likely when wolves became scavengers around human campsites and settlements.

Most dog breeds have been developed over the past one or two centuries. However, the ancestors of some of today's terriers can be traced back as early as the Roman invasion of England in 54 BCE, when Julius Caesar's legions observed small terrier type dogs being used by hunters to chase prey into underground dens and lairs. These tenacious terriers remained underground to fight and kill their quarry. This instinctive terrier behavior is called "going to earth" or "going to ground." In fact, the word *terrier* comes from the Latin word *terra*, meaning "earth."

Terrier-type dogs developed into different strains and were highly prized by their owners—and for good reason. They killed rodent pests (such as rats, mice, and gophers) in the home and on the farm. By performing this service, terriers helped prevent food loss by killing vermin that ate and contaminated stored grains and also helped reduce the spread of disease by rodents—in a time before antibiotics! Able hunters of rabbits, squirrels, and other small game, terriers could sometimes help provide for the family dinner table. Terriers provided family entertainment, too, as playful pets in the home, as tough competitors and ratters in the sporting pit, or as loving companion lapdogs in the parlor. Some things never change. Then, as now, terriers were excellent watchdogs. They are very vocal and eager to alert their owners whenever strangers approach or something is

wrong. Best of all, terriers were, and still are, considered part of the family.

HISTORY OF THE BREED

One of the best ways to learn accurate details about a breed's history is to research the oldest literature and sources available. This is because the authors were often dog breeders themselves who were alive during the formative stages of the breed and knew breeders and their animals during that historic time.

A dog breed is not created overnight, and clearly a variety of terrier-type dogs were selected and bred for many years to create the Yorkshire Terrier breed that exists today. We may not have complete written records and descriptions of all the Yorkshire Terrier's ancestors, but we do know something about the kinds of dogs that contributed to the creation of the Yorkshire Terrier breed.

It is widely accepted that terrier ancestors of the Yorkshire Terrier originated in Scotland. Terriers were named according to their region of origin, their owners' names, or the type of work they did. They had a variety of names: Waterside, Scotch, Black-and-Tan, Skye, Clydesdale, Paisley, Broken-Haired Scotch, Rosneath, Silk-coated Skye, and Glasgow, to name only a few. Many of these terriers were similar in size, shape, weight, and appearance. Some of them varied in coat type, length, texture, and color. Many of the old terrier breeds no longer exist. Others interbred and were developed into different breeds, for different purposes.

The Waterside Terrier is considered an important ancestor of today's Yorkie. It originated in the shires of Scotland and was recognized for its ratting abilities in the fields, along the canals, and in the ratting pits. In time, the breed disappeared, but before it did, it passed on many of its genes to its descendants, including the Yorkshire Terrier. It is believed that the Waterside Terrier may have contributed the genes responsible for the Yorkie's silky coat texture, blue-and-tan color, small size, and keen ratting ability.

Clydesdale, Paisley, and Skye Terriers were descendants of the Rosneath Terriers. Based on information and descriptions in the old literature, some of these breeds are also considered the foundation breeds of today's Yorkshire Terrier.

Terriers accompanied their Scottish owners when they came to England, seeking

work in the mines and textile mills. Breeders from the West Riding and Lancashire areas of Yorkshire, England, are credited with "creating" the Yorkshire Terrier breed, during a turbulent time in history. These areas were adapting to the rapid changes and rise in population brought on by the Industrial Revolution, as well as the hardships and struggles of the Luddite movement. Amidst the turmoil, the Yorkshire Terrier, and many other terrier breeds, originated.

For a detailed history of the Yorkshire Terrier breed that goes far beyond the scope of this pet manual, *The Complete Yorkshire Terrier*, by Gordon and Bennett, is highly recommended. These Yorkie experts believe the cultivation of the Yorkshire Terrier breed *can* be traced, and they describe in great detail various terriers and their possible contributions to the creation of the Yorkshire Terrier breed.

As we continue to develop new DNA tests for dogs, we are better able to trace their ancestry. DNA tests may soon give us more information about the Yorkie's family history.

The dog acknowledged as the starting point of the Yorkshire Terrier breed, the "original Yorkie," so to speak, is Huddersfield Ben, although at the time Ben was alive, the Yorkshire Terrier was not yet recognized as a breed. In fact, when Ben was exhibited, he was classified as a Broken-Haired Scotch Terrier. Sadly, Ben was run over and killed in a carriage accident in 1871, but in his short life he made an indelible mark on the Yorkshire Terrier breed. We have a good idea of Ben's appearance from photographs taken after he was restored by a taxidermist and displayed

in a glass case. But more important, from the old literature we have Ben's pedigree and descriptions of some of his close relatives.

Americans were in love with Yorkies from the first time the little dogs crossed the Atlantic Ocean and set paws on the continent. As early as 1883, Yorkies appeared in the National American Kennel Club Stud Book, which was taken over by the American Kennel Club (AKC) the following year. Americans were the first to recognize Yorkies as an official breed, to exhibit them in specific Yorkshire Terrier classes, and to award them championship titles. From 1900 to 1920, 45 Yorkshire Terriers became champions in the United States.

As Yorkies rapidly rose in popularity, many people became Yorkie breeders. In 1919, the Yorkshire Terrier Association was formed, but it lasted only a few years. In 1954, the

The Early Years

	America	England
Yorkshire Terriers recognized as an official breed	1885	1886
Yorkies exhibited under the breed name of Yorkshire Terriers	1878	1886
Yorkshire Terriers won a championship title	1889*	1897
Championship title	1905	

*The year 1889 was when the first championship title was awarded after the AKC was established. However, other Yorkies gained championship titles in New York in the early 1880s, and in 1905 the first American-bred Yorkie gained her championship title.

Yorkshire Terrier Club of America was formed.

At the time of its importation, the Yorkie was a sign of status, prestige, and high society to many—and such glamour sold for high prices. Yorkshire Terriers were considered cuddly companions to pamper, groom, carry about, travel with, exhibit, and love. More importance was given to companionship, conformation, and coat quality than to the animal's original purpose: to hunt small game and kill vermin. It was a new world, a new era, and a new lifestyle for the little toy terrier that was destined to rank as one of the most popular breeds in America.

THE YORKSHIRE TERRIER STANDARD

Today's Yorkshire Terrier has not changed much since it was first declared an official breed in 1885. The Yorkshire Terrier still moves in a proud and confident manner. Its moderately long, beautiful, glossy, fine, straight, silky coat remains a distinctive feature of the breed, although at the origin

of the breed the coat texture was reported to be less silky and more harsh than today's coat.

Coat color is still an important factor in the animal's overall quality. The blue coloration that extends from the back of the neck, over the body to the base of the tail should be a dark, metallic, steel blue, and not silvery. There should not be other colors mingled in the blue hairs. Note: Puppies are very dark at birth. The almost black coloration can take as much as two years to gradually lighten to the desired steel-blue color.

The head, chest, and legs are a deep, rich golden tan. The hair on the head, called the "fall," is long, pulled up, and tied in the center or parted in the middle and tied in two parts. The coat is parted from the base of the skull to the end of the tail, hanging straight and even on each side of a well-balanced and

compact body. The head is small and somewhat flat on top. The skull should not be rounded. The teeth meet in a scissors bite or a level bite. Eyes are medium sized and dark. The ears are small, V-shaped, and carried erect. Legs should be straight, with a moderate bend to the stifles. Feet should be round. The nose, eyelid margins, and toenails are black. A Yorkshire Terrier must not weigh more than 7 pounds (3.18 kg).

A more detailed version of the Yorkshire Terrier Breed Standard may be obtained from the American Kennel Club.

It might come as a surprise to learn that the AKC does not place the Yorkshire Terrier in the Terrier Group. The Yorkshire Terrier, with its diminutive size, is a member of the Toy Group. The toy group consists of several small breeds from a wide variety of origins,

appearances, and abilities. What this petite pooch group shares in common is small size and big personality.

Your Yorkie may be a tiny toy, but she's still a terrier—and like all terriers, she can be tough and tenacious. It is her instinctive nature to be as feisty and fearless as her larger cousins. In fact, often the smaller the Yorkie, the tougher she thinks she is!

FAMOUS YORKIES

Yorkies have warmed many laps and brightened many lives, including those of political leaders and entertainers. And Yorkies have been entertainers themselves. But the Yorkie most deserving of recognition is Smoky, considered by many to be the most famous dog of World War II. She belonged to William Wynne of Ohio, who served in the Air

Force and found the 4-pound stray in New Guinea in 1944. Wynne trained Smoky to run communication wire through a culvert under a runway to make it operational during World War II. For her work she became a war hero. Smoky also won a Best Mascot award. After the war she returned to Ohio with Mr. Wynne, who wrote a book about her titled *Yorkie Doodle Dandy* (1996).

Many Yorkshire Terriers have earned their place in the spotlight: in the show ring, obedience ring, agility, military service, pet-facilitated therapy, and community service. All these animals have done their part to bring attention to the breed and to make the Yorkshire Terrier one of the most popular dog breeds in the world.

Of course, the biggest celebrity of all is the loyal Yorkie that lives in *your* home and sits on *your* lap. She gives you unlimited and unconditional love. All she needs in return is excellent care—and this book is about how

to give your Yorkie the very best care you possibly can—so you both can share many long, happy, healthy years together.

Considerations Before You Buy a Yorkshire Terrier

The Yorkie breed has stolen your heart, but don't let it rob you of your senses as well. Don't be an impulse buyer! This dynamic diminutive dog is not for everyone. When it comes to Yorkies, small actually means "really big": big attitude, big responsibilities, and big investments of emotion, time, and money.

There is a lot to learn and think about before you can know for sure whether a Yorkshire Terrier is the right dog for you. And if you decide that a Yorkie is the perfect match for you—get ready! You are about to enjoy many years of love, fun, and companionship from the world's most wonderful and beloved terrier.

IS A YORKSHIRE TERRIER THE RIGHT DOG FOR YOU?

The Yorkshire Terrier is a very special dog, and it takes a very special kind of person to understand it, socialize it, train it, and care for it. Yorkies have behavioral and genetic (inherited) terrier traits that are deeply ingrained in this independent, overly confident little canine. After all, the Yorkie is first and foremost a terrier—active, brave, territorial, and a fierce hunter of small prey. In essence, the Yorkie is a big dog in a tiny package. He is instinctively on the lookout for vermin to chase, rodents to kill, and other adversaries to destroy. But in today's world of cities and apartment living, these instincts must be expressed in a different way. These instincts are what naturally drive Yorkies to dig, explore, bark, and sometimes shake, shred, and demolish objects. Yorkies are quick to bark warning alarms, to run and jump (often on and off furniture), and to patrol the premises.

Well known for their big-dog persona, tiny Yorkies think they are giants. An overdose of boldness, combined with their love for adventure, never-ending curiosity, and terrier tenaciousness, can be a recipe for disaster. Your Yorkie can get himself into some potentially dangerous situations, such as a confrontation with a dog 10 times his size. But being a terrier, your Yorkie probably won't back down from danger. Yorkies are not pushovers. They can be fearless to a fault and will not be intimidated.

Yorkies bond very strongly to their owners and do very well in a "one-person" family, so they are ideal for adults, older children, and some elderly people. Yorkies are not suitable for very small children because they can injure each other. Yorkies can be dropped or stepped on by children. Also, Yorkies resent rough handling and may bite if provoked. Although he will adapt to all family members, a Yorkie usually bonds most closely with one person, his caregiver.

In many ways, Yorkie puppies are like small children. They are everywhere and into

Are You Ready for a Yorkshire Terrier?

1. Would you enjoy the company of a high-energy, inquisitive little dog?
2. Do you have time to take a dog out several times a day for walks?
3. Do you have time to groom your dog and keep his coat in top condition?
4. Do you have the patience, skill, and time to train a bright little terrier with a mind and will of his own?
5. Can you forgive a little dog for instinctive behaviors, such as digging holes, shredding things, and barking?
6. Can you teach a dog, with kindness, that *you* are the boss, or "pack leader"?
7. Can you "dog-proof" your home and make it safe, to prevent injury and escape?
8. Can you meet the challenges of house training a puppy?
9. Can you afford food, supplies, and grooming for a Yorkshire Terrier?
10. Can you afford veterinary care for a Yorkshire Terrier throughout its entire long life?

lot of socialization, training, and supervision if they are to become good canine citizens. And if Yorkies do not receive fair, consistent discipline when needed, they can develop behavior problems, such as nipping or continual yapping. Misbehavior is one of the main reasons Yorkies end up in animal shelters. If you are going to own a Yorkie, you absolutely must take the time to properly raise and train him. This means you must learn how to communicate with your Yorkie in a kind, firm way that he understands (see How To: Basic Training).

Yorkshire Terriers are highly intelligent and have excellent memories. They are determined, very active busybodies. These characteristics make training and living with a Yorkie fun, entertaining, and surprising!

THE COMMITMENT TO YOUR YORKIE

Dog ownership is a joy, but it is also a big responsibility. During the years, your Yorkie will rely on you for love, attention, socialization, training, the right nutrition, regular grooming, and good health care. And with good health care, Yorkies can live up to 15 years, sometimes longer.

everything all the time. In fact, if it's too quiet in the house, be suspicious. It usually means your Yorkie is getting into trouble.

Your Yorkie may be jealous of the attention you show other people and animals, because he wants *all* of your attention *all* of the time. In fact, Yorkies can be very demanding. They can be easily spoiled. Yorkies must receive a

More Important Things to Consider Before You Make the Final Decision

Prepare the Family: Teach children responsibility and respect for animal life. Teach children the correct way to approach and handle your Yorkie so he is not injured from being dropped or stepped on. Be careful that elderly people in the home do not trip and fall over your Yorkie running underfoot.

Allergies: Make sure no one in the family has allergies to animal hair and dander. Consult your physician.

Prepare the House: Select a safe area to house the new arrival. Remove anything breakable, toxic, electrical, or valuable.

Home Schedules: Set aside time to feed, groom, exercise, and play with your Yorkie. Do not leave your Yorkie alone for long periods of time. A bored, lonely, or shut-in Yorkshire Terrier will soon find some way to entertain himself, and that usually means getting into mischief!

Vacations: Leash-train and socialize your Yorkie so he can accompany you on vacation. Otherwise, make arrangements for live-in home care for him (preferable to a boarding facility) and daily exercise.

Expenses: Plan for routine expenses (dog food, health care, supplies, grooming) and keep a savings fund for unforeseen veterinary medical emergencies.

Prepare the Yard: Make sure the yard is safely enclosed and gates latch securely. Remove poisonous plants. Buy a pool cover to prevent drowning.

Responsible Dog Ownership: License your Yorkie. Enroll in a dog training class. Vaccinate your Yorkie. Join a dog club.

Don't be misled by the Yorkie's tiny size. Small does not mean cheaper or easier to raise. Yorkies cost just as much as large dogs to own, perhaps even more. Although Yorkies eat less, they have special nutritional needs to meet their high activity level, fast metabolism, and to promote coat growth, so they need the very best food and care you can provide.

The gorgeous, flowing, silky coat for which Yorkies are famous is high maintenance. Regular grooming is an absolute must for every Yorkie and an essential part of skin, coat, and health care. *If you cannot commit to regular grooming, then a Yorkie is definitely not for you!*

Yorkies are very active and need daily exercise and enough space to run and play. Yorkies want someone to play *with* them.

When people purchase a puppy, they often do not consider that dogs are "senior citizens" at about seven years of age. If your Yorkie lives to be 15, as many Yorkies do, he will be a "senior citizen" for half of his life. Older dogs need more frequent veterinary care, such as examinations and dental cleaning, as they age. Clearly, owning and caring for a Yorkshire Terrier is a long-term commitment! Prolonged or repeated boredom or isolation can lead to separation anxiety and unwanted behavior such as continual barking, destructive chewing, digging, and soiling in the house. Fun activities and daily exercise are important.

Yorkies, like all dogs, need good medical care. Yorkies have special health care issues that need to be addressed, such as the need for frequent professional dental cleaning. And because of their tiny size, Yorkies are prone to more medical emergencies than some breeds. In short, veterinary care for a Yorkie costs no less than for any other breed.

Caring for a Yorkshire Terrier takes patience, understanding, love, time, and money. But, it is also lots of fun! So if you can make the commitment, you've made the decision of a lifetime.

Now it's time to think about when to introduce a Yorkshire Terrier into your life and home. You can start your search for the perfect puppy now, by contacting breeders and being placed on a waiting list. Don't buy the first puppy you see. Take time to prepare your home for the new arrival and to learn more about the breed, meet breeders, attend some dog shows, and join a dog club. Finding just the right dog takes time, so don't be in a

hurry. The perfect match for you is out there, and it's well worth the wait. You'll know him when you find him.

Any major changes in your life, such as relocating, a birth in the family, changing jobs, or taking a vacation, are good reasons to temporarily postpone acquiring your Yorkie. Wait until you can spend time with your new little friend and give him the care and attention he deserves.

For Yorkie's Sake!

• Do not buy a Yorkshire Terrier during the holidays. A puppy can be overlooked or neglected during the busy holidays.
• Do not transport a Yorkshire Terrier in hot or cold weather. Shipping stress causes illness, and even death, especially in young Yorkies.
• Do not buy a Yorkshire Terrier that is less than eight weeks of age. It is too young to leave the breeder or be transported.

Your Yorkshire Terrier is full of energy and curiosity. He is interested in meeting all the new members of your family, including your other pets. Play it safe! Make sure introductions are done slowly, safely, and under direct supervision. Never leave any of your pets together, even for a moment, if you are not present.

If you own another dog or a cat, don't expect them to be friends right away. They will be cautious and possibly jealous of the new arrival. A resentful dog's sharp teeth can inflict serious wounds, and eye damage, caused by cat scratches, is a common puppy injury. Yorkies may act tough, but they are small and delicate, and their bones are fragile. They can be easily injured. Keep your puppy safe.

A good way to start introductions in the family is to place your Yorkie in an area of the home where he is safe from other animals but where they can observe and smell each other. A space in the living room or den may be a good place to put a baby-barrier gate to prevent the new arrival from running loose in the house. Don't buy collapsing or folding barriers, because your Yorkie can be caught or crushed in them.

A travel kennel (crate) is an excellent training tool, if used correctly. In the beginning, place your pet in his kennel only for very short time periods. He should feel happy and secure in his kennel. He should not feel lonely and abandoned.

In most cases, animals learn to live together in a household peacefully. However, many Yorkshire Terriers insist on being top dog and will dominate the others, even if they are many times his size.

And anything smaller than a Yorkie will surely fall prey to it, especially small mammals. Small pets are no match for your Yorkie's hunting prowess.

Make sure the lid or door to your small pet's cage is securely fastened. Then place the cage where your Yorkie cannot find it or reach it.

GOOD REASONS TO NEUTER YOUR YORKIE

Deciding to neuter your Yorkie is one of the most important health decisions you will ever make for him.

Neutering ("spay" for females, "castration" for males) is a surgical procedure in which reproductive organs are removed (ovaries and uterus in the female, testicles in the male) so that the animal cannot reproduce and will not develop infections or cancer in these organs in later years.

Yorkshire Terriers can reach sexual maturity and be able to reproduce as early as six months of age, although at this age they are not completely mature.

The best time to neuter a Yorkie is when he has grown up enough to safely tolerate the anesthesia and surgical procedure.

Benefits of neutering females
• prevent unwanted pregnancies
• eliminate inconveniences associated with estrus (vaginal bleeding, discharge that stains furniture and carpets and attracts neighborhood dogs)
• prevent cancer of the ovaries and uterus
• help prevent mammary (breast) cancer if spayed before first estrus

Benefits of neutering males
• prevent cancer of testicles and epididymis
• reduce prostate problems
• reduce behavior problems

Every Yorkshire Terrier is different, and his medical care should be determined on an individual basis. Consult your veterinarian about the health benefits and possible risks of neutering your Yorkie, the best time to do the procedure, and any other concerns you may have about your pet.

Selecting Your Yorkshire Terrier

Yorkshire Terriers have become victims of their enormous popularity. Because Yorkies are in such high demand, many people raise Yorkies hoping to "get rich quick," without regard for a Yorkie's special needs or genetic makeup. Beware of these sellers. The very best way to find a high-quality Yorkie is to buy from a reputable Yorkie breeder.

WHERE TO FIND A PUPPY, ADOLESCENT, OR ADULT?

Buy your Yorkshire Terrier from a reputable breeder. The best way to find a reputable breeder is to contact your local or national Yorkshire Terrier association (see Information) to help you find a respected and knowledgeable Yorkie breeder. The Yorkshire Terrier Club of America can also give you information about Yorkie clubs, shows, and events.

Word of mouth is a good way to find a top breeder. Join a breed, or all-breed, dog club in your area so you can meet breeders, dog trainers, and professional dog show handlers and get their recommendations.

A reputable breeder will also ask you questions and ask for references, including your veterinarian's name and contact information.

Don't let your passion for puppies interfere with your good judgment. Always ask for references and obtain health guarantees in writing. *Decide first on the breeder, then decide on the puppy.*

Nothing is cuter than a Yorkie puppy, but puppyhood is brief, so don't base your decision simply on appearance and age. When looking for the ideal companion, the most important considerations are health and personality.

A Yorkie's personality is well established by the time she is 12 weeks of age. By obtaining a puppy in the early stages of her life, you can positively influence her adult personality and behavioral development. This is much easier than trying to change an established undesirable behavior in an adult dog.

Picking the Perfect Puppy

To make sure all goes well with your puppy purchase, here is a checklist of documents and information to obtain from the breeder.

1. Health guarantee from the breeder and other contractual information such as spay/neuter agreements, return and refund policies, sales contracts, and sales receipt.

2. Health certificate from a veterinarian.

3. Medical record listing all vaccines and treatments the puppy has received.

4. Microchip identification number and forms for the new owner to register with the microchip database.

5. Kennel club registration application form or transfer of ownership form, signed by the breeder. Check whether your puppy has limited registration or full registration.

6. Pedigree listing the names, titles, and other information about the dog's family.

7. Written care instructions from the breeder, including feeding instructions and recommended diet.

There are also many advantages to purchasing an older Yorkie. The breeder will have already socialized and trained her. She will be leash trained and house-trained. In general, Yorkies are very adaptable dogs, but it might take a while for your new friend to feel completely at home with a new family and change of lifestyle.

Tiny Dog, Big Problems

Do not buy "teacup," "miniature," or "doll face" Yorkies, or adult Yorkies weighing 3 pounds or less. These runts usually have health problems, genetic defects, and malformations. They need medical care and have short life spans. They are poor specimens of the Yorkshire Terrier breed. Reputable breeders do not breed or raise them.

Male or Female?

Both male and female Yorkshire Terriers make wonderful companions. Every Yorkie has its own unique personality, so it's not accurate or fair to make a generalized statement about whether males or females have the best temperaments or make the best pets. It all depends on your personal preferences and your Yorkie's environmental influences, genetic traits, learned behaviors, and training.

Male Yorkies can be very territorial and "mark" their territory by lifting a leg and

Always Buy from a Reputable Breeder!

Do not buy a Yorkie from a puppy mill.

Puppy mills mass-produce puppies and cut corners on their care, nutrition, and hygiene. Puppies from these sellers are poor specimens of the breed. They usually have been raised in dirty, cramped conditions and often have health problems and genetic defects. "Puppy mills" often sell pups to pet stores undernourished, heavily parasitized, and not socialized. *Reputable breeders interview, screen, and carefully select their puppies' future owners and keep track of their puppies throughout their lives.*

urinating—frequently. Neutering at a young age may help reduce this tendency. Males can also take longer to house-train than females. Female Yorkies try to be the "alpha" or dominant animal.

One or More?

Advantages

- More fun and surprises.
- You will always have Yorkie companionship.
- Yorkies can keep each other company and play together and can take walks together.

Drawbacks

- More time and work: training, grooming, cleaning.
- More expense: food, health care, supplies, and grooming.
- Yorkies may be jealous of each other, or they may bond more closely to each other than with you.
- Yorkies may need different diets and may have to be separated when fed.

Show Dog or Companion Only?

A Yorkshire Terrier destined for the show ring must adhere closely to the breed standard and be an outstanding representative of the breed. A companion Yorkie may have minor imperfections with regard to the high conformation standards of a future champion but be wonderful in all other respects. Usually the differences between a champion and a nonchampion Yorkie are obvious only to the trained eye of a dog show judge or an experienced breeder. They in no way diminish the animal's value as a loving member of the family.

If you are bitten by the show bug and must purchase a show dog, be prepared to pay more for it than you would for a pet-quality companion. And if you buy a puppy

Yorkie Puppy Health

✔ **Attitude:** Healthy, alert, playful, inquisitive, eager to greet you

✔ **Eyes:** Bright; clear; free of discharge, tearing, and staining

✔ **Ears:** Clean; free of parasites, dirt, and wax; no head shaking or scratching

✔ **Mouth:** Gums bright pink, teeth properly aligned

✔ **Skin and Coat:** Healthy, glossy, clean, with no parasites or sores, no mats or knots, no soiling or diarrhea under the tail

✔ **Tail and Dewclaws:** Dewclaws have been removed and tail has been docked* (top two-thirds removed)

✔ **Body Condition:** Full body, not too thin, and does not have a distended or bloated belly

✔ **Movement:** Normal gait for a puppy; moves freely and willingly; no limping, hopping, or skipping

*These procedures are done at three to five days of age. If done later in life, they require anesthesia and pain relievers. Tail docking is not permissible in some countries that consider the procedure unnecessary and inhumane.

Coat of Changing Colors

Your Yorkie puppy's coat is much darker than that of her parents. Yorkshire Terriers are born very dark in color. Their coats gradually lighten to the beautiful deep steel blue and rich tan colors of an adult.

National Parent Club

The National Parent Club, the Yorkshire Terrier Club of America (*www.theyorkshireterrierclubofamerica.org*) is an excellent source of information for Yorkshire Terrier owners. It provides information on the breed, the detailed breed standard, show information, educational opportunities activities to do with your Yorkshire Terrier, ethics, guidelines, articles, membership information, and much more.

as a "show prospect," there is no guarantee that it will turn out to be a champion, even if its parents are champions. If you really want to win in the conformation ring, consider buying an adult Yorkie that has already been successful at the shows. It will be hard to find one for sale, but once in a while a great opportunity presents itself. Be prepared to pay for it.

AGE AND LONGEVITY

Small breeds live longer than large breeds, and Yorkshire Terriers live a long time! With good nutrition and excellent care a Yorkie may live up to 15 years or more. So choose your new companion wisely. You and your

Yorkie are going to be together for many years.

Full Registration

This type of registration is for show dogs and breeding animals. It allows for participation in AKC conformation class, competitions, and events, and makes it possible to register future offspring of the animal with the AKC.

Limited Registration

Dogs that are sold as pets, and not for show or breeding, should be sold with a limited registration. Dogs with limited registration cannot be used for breeding, and if they are bred, their offspring cannot be registered with the AKC. Dogs with limited registration cannot compete in conformation classes, but they can compete in other AKC events, such as obedience and agility. Only the dog's breeder (not

Yorkie Expenses

The cost of Yorkshire Terrier ownership can add up quickly. Here are some things to consider

✔ **Food:** Yorkshire Terriers require top-quality nutrition. Dog food prices vary according to brand, quality, and region, and prices continue to rise. Prescription diets are more expensive.

✔ **Veterinary care:** Depends on the age, sex, health, and lifestyle of your pet. Veterinary fees vary; specialists' fees are higher. Laboratory tests, surgery, or medical emergency can cost hundreds to thousands of dollars. Many Yorkshire Terriers need frequent dental cleaning and polishing. Even a healthy dog needs an annual examination, routine laboratory tests, and vaccinations.

Note: The American Kennel Club offers a health insurance program for dogs.

✔ **Accessories:** Crate, exercise pen, collar, leash, bed, dishes, toys, grooming supplies.

✔ **Travel:** Additional fee plus deposit, for hotels that accept dogs.

✔ **Boarding facility or pet sitter fees:** For times when you cannot take your Yorkie with you when you travel.

✔ **Dog license:** Varies according to county and state.

✔ **Liability insurance:** Varies according to insurance company.

An Informed Owner

✔ Begin the search for your Yorkshire Terrier by contacting the Yorkshire Terrier Club of America and local breed clubs, visiting dog shows, and contacting reputable, respected breeders.

✔ Learn as much as you can about the Yorkshire Terrier breed, talk to breeders, and ask them questions.

✔ Decide whether to purchase a puppy, adolescent, or adult Yorkie.

✔ Remember that health and personality are the key considerations.

✔ Obtain all relevant documents at the time of purchase.

the owner) can change a dog's status from limited registration to full registration.

HELP! WHAT ABOUT RESCUE?

Many Yorkies end up in animal shelters or with rescue groups. Most are adults that have been relinquished because of behavior problems, usually related to failure to be housetrained. Barking, destructive behavior, separation anxiety, and biting are also high on the problem list. Many of these Yorkies also have health and genetic problems. Some Yorkies have simply been abandoned because their original owners didn't have time for them.

Giving a Yorkie a second chance in life is challenging, but can be very rewarding. If you have the patience, time, knowledge, and finances to provide a home for a Yorkie in need, the Yorkshire Terrier Club of America and other groups (see Information) can put you in touch with a rescue coordinator.

Yorkie Quick Reference Chart		
	High	**Moderate**
Grooming Needs	✗	
Intelligence, Trainability	✗	
Watchdog Ability	✗	
Protective, Territorial	✗	
Bonds with One Owner	✗	
Energy Level	✗	
Mind of Its Own	✗	
Ease of Spoiling	✗	
Challenges Authority	✗	
Friendliness (with Strangers)		✗

At Home with Your Yorkshire Terrier

You have found the perfect Yorkie and now it's time to bring him home. Everything must be perfect for the new arrival to keep him safe and secure!

Yorkshire Terriers, especially baby Yorkies, like to feel comfortable and safe. Yorkies are quick to adapt, and you can make the transition period easy and stress-free for your puppy and yourself by being well prepared before bringing your new little friend home.

YOUR YORKIE COMES HOME

The first step in preparing your Yorkie for the trip home is to get him used to a travel kennel. This is usually done by the breeder, in anticipation of your puppy's future trip home with you. Most breeders introduce their puppies to a travel kennel when they are very young, so they can play and sleep in it and use it as a "den."

The first trip will set the travel rules for years to follow. If you hold your puppy on your lap, he will expect to be outside the travel kennel on every trip. A dog that is loose in the car is a distraction and can cause an accident, or be tossed about and seriously injured in an accident.

Leave your Yorkie in the travel kennel where he is safe while you are driving or traveling in the car.

Car sickness is common in young Yorkies. Your Yorkie may drool, vomit, or defecate, so be sure to bring along plenty of disposable towels and a plastic bag. Your puppy will outgrow his car sickness faster if you take him on short car trips on a regular basis. Reward him with a small treat and play with him after each trip.

When you first bring your Yorkie home, give him a little quiet time, some food, and a drink of water. Yorkie puppies have fast metabolisms. They burn up calories very quickly and they tire quickly. They need a lot of sleep. If there are children in the home, teach them to respect naptime. Children's shrill voices and sudden movements can startle a tiny puppy.

It is very important to teach children in the home the proper way to lift and handle your Yorkie, by gently putting one hand under his chest and the other under his hindquarters for support. Small children should remain seated, preferably on the floor, when petting or handling a Yorkie, so they do not drop or injure the animal.

Supervise children at all times when they are holding a Yorkie!

Most Yorkie injuries—broken bones and head trauma—are caused by being dropped or stepped on.

Never lift a Yorkie by the scruff of the neck or by the limbs.

Naming Your Yorkie

Your Yorkie's personality will shine through, and it won't be difficult for you to think of the perfect name that matches his personality.

If you cannot think of a good name, dog name books are available that list hundreds of names and their meanings (see Information). It won't take long for your Yorkie to learn his name. In fact, he will not only know when you are talking *to* him, but will also know when you are talking *about* him!

HOUSING AND SAFETY CONSIDERATIONS

Ever since their early history, Yorkshire Terriers have been indoor dogs. They may have spent hours in the fields hunting and killing vermin, but when they were not working, they were safely tucked away in the home. In fact, tucked away is a good way to describe their housing. In England during the 1800s, Yorkies were housed in boxes kept under the table, or in kitchen cupboards. The cupboard doors were replaced with wire mesh or bars so that the dogs could observe family activities in the kitchen. Sometimes the animals' quarters

Convenient Housing Options

Travel Kennels: Ideal for small dog-house, lightweight, easy to clean and disinfect, well ventilated, draft-free, private.

Exercise Pens (X-pens): Available in a variety of sizes, attachments for dishes and bottles, optional fitted wire tops.

Safety Gates: Close off areas and stairways to prevent escape or injury. Do not use folding barriers or gates that can collapse, fold, trap, and injure Yorkies.

Bedding: Bedding should be natural material (cotton, wool). Some synthetic materials or cedar shavings can cause allergies.

Yorkie Collars

Yorkies are so small that cat break-away collars may be safer and more suitable for them than buckle dog collars. For Yorkies that have tracheal collapse problems, harnesses are recommended. Check your pet's collar daily to be sure it fits properly.

were stacked or tiered. Today's Yorkie is much more fortunate. He is often given full run of the house and allowed to sit on the furniture, and if he is especially spoiled, he may even sleep in his owner's bed!

When Yorkies are not outside exploring, taking a walk, or playing, they should always be housed inside where they are safe and can be supervised.

Location

Before you bring your puppy home, decide on a place to house him (an X-pen, or an area blocked off from, but near, the family room or living room) where he is safe and you can observe him. Choose wisely, because this area may eventually become your pet's permanent housing and sleeping quarters. Yorkshire Terriers want to be the center of attention. They also want to be in the center of all activities. But being everywhere all the time is not safe, especially for a new puppy. And just like people, Yorkies need privacy and quiet time. A travel kennel is ideal for use as a den and gives a

sense of security without isolating your pet from the family.

Exposure to various sights, sounds, smells, activities, and people are all an important part of Yorkie socialization. Your puppy doesn't know the rules yet, so make sure his space is in an area where he cannot chew electrical wires, baseboards, or furniture, and cannot urinate on the carpet.

If you have acquired an older Yorkshire Terrier, try to duplicate the previous housing situation as much as possible to reduce the stress of changing environments.

Many of the things you love most about your Yorkie—his tiny size, high activity level, and curiosity—also make him accident-prone. Before your Yorkie comes home, do a safety

Yorkie Necessities

- ✔ Travel kennel
- ✔ Comfortable sleeping quarters and dog bed or big pillow cushion
- ✔ Food and water dishes, water bottles with sipper tubes
- ✔ High-quality puppy/dog food recommended by the breeder or veterinarian
- ✔ Lightweight cat collar
- ✔ Dog harness for walks (ideal for safe, fast pickup in case of emergency)
- ✔ Leash (retractable-style is not recommended)
- ✔ Sweater for warmth
- ✔ Grooming and dental supplies (see Grooming Your Yorkie)
- ✔ First aid kit
- ✔ Exercise pen (X-pen), safety gate, or other safe, escape-proof enclosure
- ✔ Safe, chew-proof toys

check and "Yorkie-proof" your home by removing all potential hazards from your diminutive friend.

Make sure your home is safe before you let your Yorkshire Terrier go exploring.

Supervise your Yorkie at all times.

Household Cleaning Products and Chemicals

Because your Yorkie is so small, it takes only a small amount of toxic substances to kill him. Keep cleaning products and chemicals out of your pet's reach.

Antifreeze

Antifreeze (ethylene glycol) is a common cause of animal poisoning. It can be found on garage floors and has a sweet taste that attracts animals. A very small amount can cause permanent, severe kidney damage.

Rodent Poisons and Snap Traps

Rodent bait is deadly for all animals. If your Yorkie consumes rodent bait or eats a poisoned rodent, he will be poisoned as well.

If you have set snap traps in your house or garage, remove them. They can easily break a Yorkie's tiny toes or injure a nose.

Electrical Shock

Make sure your Yorkie cannot reach or chew on electrical cords. Electrocution from gnawing on an electrical cord could cost your pet his life and possibly cause an electrical fire.

Kitchen and Appliances

Many pets have been seriously burned by hot liquids spilled from pots on the stove. Don't let your Yorkie run around your feet in the kitchen while you are cooking.

Doors

Make sure all doors to the outside and to the garage are closed. If your pet escapes outdoors, he can become lost, stolen, hit by an automobile, or injured by wildlife and neighborhood dogs.

The garage is a dangerous place for a Yorkie. He could gain access to stored toxic chemicals or be hurt by sharp tools.

Be careful when closing doors. Many Yorkie injuries and broken bones are caused by being caught in closing doors.

Injuries

Yorkie ownership means learning to shuffle your feet! One of the most common Yorkie injuries is broken bones resulting from being accidentally stepped on by a family member.

Another common Yorkie injury is trauma from being dropped. Even a few feet is a skydive fall for a little Yorkie, and those delicate bones break easily. Handle with care!

Poisonous Plants

Most ornamental plants are toxic to animals. Yorkshire Terriers have a natural instinct to dig, explore, and chew. Keep household plants out of reach, and limit home and garden plants to nontoxic varieties.

Fertilizers and Mulch

Lawn and garden fertilizers are poisonous to dogs. Do not use cocoa mulch or fertilizers in areas of your yard where your pet plays.

Foreign Objects

Dogs explore with their mouths and swallow unusual things. Make sure small balls, children's toys, rubber bands, paper clips, pens, coins, and all other unsafe objects are out of reach. Pennies contain high levels of zinc and can cause zinc poisoning. Be sure that the toys you purchase are safe. Avoid toys with small pieces, buttons, bells, or whistles that may be a choking hazard.

Garbage

"Garbage poisoning" is common and can cause death. It is caused by spoiled and decaying foods that are contaminated with bacteria that produce toxins and cause poisoning. In addition, dogs that rummage through the garbage often eat paper wrappers, plastic wrap, aluminum foil, bones, and other objects that can cause intestinal obstruction. Keep your Yorkie out of the trash!

Candies, Medicines, and Foods

Candies and medicines are dangerous for Yorkies. An overdose of common medicines, including aspirin and ibuprofen, can be fatal. Chocolate contains a methylxanthine sub-stance (theobromine) similar to caffeine that is toxic to dogs. Some artificial sweeteners, such as Xylitol, found in human foods, gum, and candies are toxic to dogs. Hard candies can become lodged between the teeth at the back of the jaw or be a serious choking hazard.

Grapes and raisins are toxic to dogs and can cause acute kidney failure. Macadamia nuts are also poisonous to dogs.

IDENTIFICATION

Have your pet permanently identified as soon as possible.

Microchips

One of the best forms of animal identifi-cation is a microchip. A microchip is a tiny transponder about the size of a grain of rice. It is implanted under the skin quickly and easily by injection. The microchip identifica-tion numbers are read by a handheld scanner. Microchips are safe, permanent, and tam-per-proof. The entire identification procedure takes only a few seconds. Scanning is abso-lutely painless and is accurate.

A central computer registry records the animal's identification number and owner information. Lost animals can be identified at animal shelters, humane societies, and veter-inary offices.

Microchip identification is one of the best things you can do for your Yorkie.

Nametags are an excellent form of iden-tification. Many pet stores offer on-the-spot nametag engraving. Tags are easily visible and let others know your lost companion has a family. *Be sure to keep a current phone number on the tag.*

HOUSE-TRAINING YOUR YORKIE

Behavior problems are the biggest reasons owners relinquish their Yorkshire Terriers to animal shelters and rescue groups, and house-training failures top the list.

Yorkies are very smart. They are also very clean. So why does it take some Yorkies a long time to become fully house-trained? Because some Yorkie owners do not know the correct way to house-train their puppies!

The secrets to successful Yorkie house-training are patience, diligence, attentiveness, consistency, making sure your puppy gets to the right place at the right time, and lots and lots of praise.

At first, you will spend a lot of time house-training your puppy. For example, because puppies have such fast metabolisms, they can make urine and feces rapidly. And because Yorkie puppies have very small urinary bladders, there is not much storage space! So, in order to prevent accidents in the home, you will have to let your puppy out to do his business every one to two hours. If the house-training assignments can be divided between family members, everyone will have a chance to sleep! As your puppy grows, he will gain more control of his bladder and bowel functions, and eventually be able to hold himself for two to three hours. Over time, as he matures, he will eventually be able to wait six hours (overnight), so your house-training efforts will not be as time-consuming.

Give your puppy several opportunities throughout the day to relieve himself, so that he does not accidentally soil in the house or develop bad toilet habits. Take him to the

Accidents

If a Yorkie (puppy or adult) is already house-trained and starts having accidents in the house, this could be a sign of medical problems such as a bladder infection. Consult your veterinarian right away.

House-training

1. Start house-training your Yorkie puppy the day he arrives.
2. Watch closely for signs that your puppy needs to urinate or defecate. Signs include acting anxiously, sniffing the ground, circling, whining, crying, or pacing.
3. Always take your puppy to the same location to eliminate. In the beginning, it may be helpful to place a small amount of your puppy's feces in the spot where you would like him to learn to eliminate.
4. Let your Yorkie out several times a day, at least every one to two hours to start. While your puppy is outside, allow him time to walk around and sniff the ground. This stimulates elimination.
5. Let your puppy out to eliminate first thing in the morning, after every meal, after drinking, after naps, after playtime, and right before bedtime.
6. Keep your puppy on a regular schedule to go outside.
7. Keep your puppy on a regular feeding schedule.
8. Make sure your puppy is free of intestinal parasites.
9. If you have another dog in the family that is already house-trained, bring it along with you to help house-train your puppy. Your puppy can learn by following your trained dog's example.
10. Never scold your Yorkie puppy if he has an accident in the house.
11. Praise your puppy profusely when he does the right thing. A small food reward after he has done his job can be a powerful positive reinforcement.
12. Be patient, understanding, kind, and consistent in your training.

same spot every time. When you need to be away from the house for a while, confine him to an X-pen and spread newspapers or "wee pads" (from the pet store) on an easy-to-clean floor. You can also train your puppy to use a litter box. Give him a shallow litter box filled with absorbent dog litter from the pet store. Put him in the box when he shows signs of impending elimination.

Until your Yorkie is fully vaccinated, do not take him outside where other dogs have gone. He may contract diseases or parasites.

A travel kennel is a valuable house-training tool, as long as it is not misused. Yorkies hate to soil their living quarters. In his travel kennel, your puppy will hold himself as long as he possibly can. This can be useful if you need to leave the house for 20 to 30 minutes. Let him out immediately upon your return and take him to the right spot to do his business.

Yorkies gain more control over their bodily functions with time. When your puppy is older, you can put him in a large travel kennel or exercise pen (X-pen) late at night and let him out first thing in the morning. Be sure to get up early. It's unfair for you to sleep in while your puppy is miserable with a full bladder.

Never use the travel crate for long-term confinement.

In spite of your diligence, there will be some "accidents." Keep in mind that these are not intentional. *Do not punish, strike, or shake your Yorkie. Do not raise your voice.* Simply say "No" and clean the soiled area well so he will not be attracted to it later. *Use positive reinforcement only. Praise your Yorkie profusely and give him a treat when he does the right thing. Be kind and patient.*

DENTAL CARE

Yorkshire Terriers are prone to dental problems and gum disease. If they do not receive regular dental care, they can quickly accumulate tartar and plaque on their teeth. Tartar and plaque start with bacterial growth and food debris on the dental surface. These

A Beautiful Smile

Retained baby teeth are common in Yorkies. If the deciduous teeth do not come out when the adult teeth grow in, teeth are overcrowded in the mouth and dental problems result. Retained deciduous teeth must be extracted!

Bad Breath

Bad breath is not normal for a dog. It is a sign of a health problem, including dental disease. If your Yorkshire Terrier has bad breath, consult your veterinarian.

harden into a brown coating, starting at the gum line. Periodontal disease develops and causes swollen, painful, bleeding gums and tooth loss. Bacteria present in the mouth and gums enter the bloodstream and can spread infection to the heart (especially the valves), liver, kidneys, and other organs. For these reasons, regular dental care is one of the most important aspects of your Yorkshire Terrier's health care program.

The best way to prevent dental disease is to brush your Yorkie's teeth. Ideally, this should be done on a daily basis and not less often than once a week. Start training your Yorkie to accept dental brushing while he is still a puppy.

Yorkie puppies are born without teeth. When they reach three to four weeks of age, their deciduous teeth (baby teeth, "milk" teeth) start to erupt. Within a few months, your Yorkie should have 28 temporary teeth. These teeth will have fallen out by the time your Yorkie is an adult, however; if you practice brushing your pup's "baby teeth," it is a great way to train your Yorkie to get used to brushing. That way, by the time your Yorkie's 48 permanent adult teeth have erupted, you and your Yorkie will have an established routine!

Brushing the Teeth

Purchase a soft-bristle toothbrush and dog toothpaste (dentifrice) recommended by your veterinarian. Do not use human toothpaste.

Start with the upper front teeth (incisors), brushing down and away from the gum line, and proceed back to the premolars and molars on each side of the mouth. You may also brush in a gentle, circular motion. Pay special attention to the upper canine teeth and molars, as plaque and tartar accumulate faster on these teeth. When you brush the bottom teeth, start with the incisors and work back to the molars, brushing up and away from the gum line.

Good home dental care is a necessity, but it is not a replacement for veterinary dental visits. Even with the best of care, most Yorkies need routine professional dental cleaning and polishing.

Toenails

Nail trimming prevents the nails from overgrowing and snagging or tearing. Overgrown nails can interfere with movement and the ability to walk correctly. In severe cases, overgrown toenails can curve under and pierce through the flesh of the foot pads.

Check to see if your Yorkie has dewclaws. These are nails found higher up on the inside of the legs. Dewclaws do not come in contact with the ground, so they do not wear down naturally. If they are not trimmed regularly, they can grow very long, or curl into the dog's flesh.

Cutting Yorkie toenails takes practice because their toenails are black. You cannot see the "quick" (where the blood supply begins).

To check if your Yorkie needs a nail trim, stand him on the grooming table. None of the nails should touch the surface of the table. Notice that each toenail curves and tapers into a point. Trim only the curved tip of the nail.

Most Yorkshire Terrier experts prefer guillotine-style clippers for adult dogs. To use these, place the toenail inside the metal loop, aligning the upper and lower blades with the area you wish to cut, and squeeze the clipper handles. If you accidentally cut too close, you can stop the bleeding by applying styptic powder or gel (available from your veterinarian or pet store) or by applying pressure with a clean cloth to the toenail for five minutes.

Replace dull blades so they do not break, shred, or crack the nails. An electric toenail filer does a nice job of rounding off and smoothing the nails after trimming.

EXERCISE AND TOYS

Yorkshire Terriers *love* to go on walks, and walking is one of the best forms of exercise for them.

Develop a healthful exercise program suitable for your Yorkie's age, stage of development, health, and physical abilities. A regular exercise program will strengthen your pet's cardiovascular system, endurance, and function. Exercise also strengthens bones and joints, and develops muscles.

Exercise Activities for Your Yorkshire Terrier

Walking: Walking is the best form of exercise for your Yorkie. Just remember that for every step you take, your Yorkie has to take several steps! A brisk walking pace for you can be full speed for a tiny Yorkie puppy. Don't overdo it. Start with short walks each day and gradually increase the distance or speed according to your pet's abilities.

Yorkie joints and bones are delicate, especially if they are young and still developing, or old and arthritic. Exercise on a soft, level surface, such as a lawn or the beach. Sidewalks and asphalt are uncomfortable and hard on the joints upon impact. They are also *very hot* during the summer. Rocky or gravel surfaces hurt tiny feet.

Check the feet for stickers, torn toenails, cuts, or abrasions after every walk. If there are sores, treat them and discontinue walks until the feet have completely healed.

Always keep your Yorkshire Terrier on a leash when you are exercising him in public to reduce the chances of loss or injury.

Catch, Fetch, and Retrieve: Many Yorkshire Terriers will chase and retrieve objects for their owners. You can use a wide variety of interesting objects for this game, including flying disks, balls, and dumbbells. Just be sure they are small enough and soft enough for your pet's tiny, tender mouth.

Yorkshire Terriers love toys. They love to "shake and kill" them, too! Toys with flapping parts, or that crackle or rattle, are especially exciting. Be sure the toys you buy are durable and safe.

Chew toys are good for the gums and exercise the jaws. Some may help reduce tartar buildup on the teeth. Chew toys are great distractions. They keep dogs busy chewing on something other than furniture and clothing.

Not all toys are suitable for Yorkies. For example, cow hooves, and elk or deer antlers, available as chew toys in local pet stores, are very hard and can cause tooth fracture. Following is a list of dangerous toys that can break, shred, or tear and become lodged in the airway passages or gastrointestinal tract.

Dangerous Toys
- Cow hooves, elk and deer antlers
- Rawhide sticks, bones, and other shapes
- Latex toys, rubber toys, cotton ropes, hard plastic toys
- Toys small enough to be swallowed
- Toys with small parts that can be swallowed (buttons, bells, squeakers)

Yorkie Playtime

Playtime is a very important part of Yorkie puppy training and socializing. It is a time for your puppy to learn some manners, too. Set aside lots of time to play with your Yorkie throughout the day. For a puppy, several short play sessions are more fun and rewarding that one very long session. Puppies need to eat, nap, and do their toilet business in between play periods.

Even tiny terriers can act tough and play rough. Sometimes overzealous play can turn into aggressive behavior. It can start with nipping, eventually escalating to snapping and biting. It is important to know the difference between normal play and unacceptable aggressive play so that you can correct your puppy immediately and teach him to play gently.

The first rule of playtime is that your Yorkie should never bite you. He should not chew on your fingers, either. If he tries to do this, say "ouch" and stop playing with him for a few minutes. Give him a "time out" by placing him in an exercise pen alone with his toys. "Time out" is a very effective training method, because more than anything your puppy wants to be with you and play with you. When he has calmed down, give him a

> **Never discipline your Yorkie by striking him, shaking him, or grabbing him by the nape of the neck.**

chance to show that he has learned his lesson and take him out to play with you again. You may even reward him with a small food treat at the end of the play period if he has been a very good playmate.

While playing with your pet, if he starts to become rambunctious and you anticipate that he might become "mouthy," distract him immediately with a toy that he can chew *before* he tries to chew on you. He will quickly divert his attention to the distraction

Normal Play Behavior
- Play bow: puppy raises rump and lowers head and wags tail
- Relaxed posture, relaxed facial expressions
- Running
- Chasing
- Pouncing
- Barking
- Growling

Aggressive Behavior
- Deep growling
- Stiff posture
- Raised hackles and tail
- Fixed staring
- Rigid posture
- Aggressive snapping and biting

and also learn that it is all right to bite and chew on toys, but that biting you is unacceptable behavior.

Give your puppy plenty of exercise and stimulating toys in between your play periods, so that he is not bored when he is alone and then overly wild or hyper-excited when playtime begins.

If you need help training your puppy or managing unacceptable behavior, consult an expert (trainer, animal behaviorist, veterinarian) for behavior counseling and help right away. The sooner the problems are correctly addressed, the better your puppy will behave and the more fun you both will have together.

TRAVELING WITH YOUR YORKIE

Yorkies love to travel, and no doubt a big part of the reason you chose this toy breed is because of its small, portable size. Surely you were planning on taking your Yorkie with you wherever and whenever you can.

Travel Tips

1. Train your Yorkie to a travel kennel early in life. Put food treats and toys in the kennel to make it more inviting.

2. Make a few short practice trips.

3. Make hotel, campground, and airline reservations well in advance and *be sure to tell them you are traveling with a pet.*

4. Make a list of everything you will need and pack early.

5. Microchip your pet and update your contact information.

6. Obtain a health certificate for out-of-state or international travel.

7. Make sure all core vaccinations are up to date, especially the rabies vaccination. Check to find out if noncore vaccinations (such as Leptospirosis or Lyme Disease) are recommended where you are going. Check with your veterinarian to learn if special mediations for the trip are recommended, such as medication for the prevention of heartworm disease or carsickness.

8. Make sure you have all the things you will need during the trip.
- Travel kennel
- Collar and harness with identification tags and leash
- Dishes, food, water bottle with sipper tube, and bottled water
- Medications
- First aid kit
- Toys and bedding from home
- Grooming supplies
- Cleanup equipment: pooper scooper, plastic bags, paper towels
- Veterinary records and photo identification

Traveling by Car

Yorkshire Terriers love to travel by car. To help prevent car sickness, limit food one hour before travel begins and, if possible and safe, place the travel kennel where your Yorkie can see out the window.

Tranquilizers are *not* recommended. Ask your veterinarian about medication for car sickness.

Never leave your Yorkshire Terrier in a parked car on a hot day, even for a few minutes. Your Yorkie cannot tolerate hot weather. The temperature inside a car, even with the windows cracked open and parked in the shade, can quickly soar past 120°F (48.9°C) within a few short minutes, and your pet can quickly die of heatstroke.

Flying with Your Yorkie

Your Yorkie is small enough to board the plane as a carry-on and fit comfortably under the seat in front of you in his travel kennel or travel bag in some planes.

Your Yorkie must be able to sit, stand, turn around, and lie down comfortably in his travel kennel.

Most airlines allow only two animals in the cabin, so make your reservation as early as possible.

Overseas travel is different. Most airlines will not allow pets in the cabin for overseas flights. There are also special requirements for dogs entering foreign countries, so check with the airlines as well as the embassies of the countries you will be visiting to be sure you have all the necessary requirements and documentation in order.

Tranquilizers are not recommended for air travel. Tranquilizers can be harmful, or even cause death, in dogs during travel at high altitudes.

DOG PARKS AND REST STOPS

Dog parks and rest stops sound like fun places for dogs to run loose and play, but your Yorkie can encounter many dangers there.

He can contract infectious diseases and high numbers of internal and external parasites from direct contact with sick animals or from contact with their feces and urine. Disease can also be spread by sharing the

same water bowls or watering areas. Fleas abound in these environments and are easily transmitted to dogs (and people!), along with their associated ills (such as diseases, skin problems, tapeworms).

Dog aggression is common at dog parks. A small Yorkie can be seriously injured by a dog attack. In addition, not all parks are adequately fenced, so there is risk of escape and possibly injury from being hit by a car.

If you decide to take your Yorkie to a park, always keep a leash and cell phone with you, in case you need to capture and leash your pet, or need to call for help.

GROOMING YOUR YORKIE

A huge part of the Yorkshire Terrier's luring appeal is his stunning, long, silky, flowing, blue-and-tan coat. But that gorgeous gown wasn't created overnight. It is a labor of love and the result of excellent health, high-quality nutrition, the right genetics, and hours of regular grooming. Brushing the coat keeps it

43

glossy and free of mats and tangles. To grow a beautiful coat, your Yorkie has to have very healthy skin, too.

Yorkies have very sensitive skin and can be prone to skin conditions and allergies. Grooming stimulates the skin, spreads natural oils, and gives you an opportunity to check for signs of dry or oily skin, and for lumps and bumps, parasites, stickers, and scabs.

The more you practice grooming, the more skilled you will be and the more handsome your Yorkie will look.

Coat Quality

Your Yorkshire Terrier inherited his coat quality, texture, and color from his parents. Without the genes to grow a fabulous show coat, all the products in the world (shampoos, rinses, nutritional supplements, brushes, and combs) will not turn an ordinary coat into a

champion show coat. There is no substitute for good genetics that can be purchased in a bottle at the pet store. A beautiful coat starts by buying a healthy, high-quality Yorkie from a reputable breeder.

Ouch! Protect the Skin!

1. Do not use harsh shampoos, chemicals, or products on your Yorkie's skin.

2. Avoid hot, dry environments that can dry out your pet's skin. Yorkies can develop itchy, flaky skin during the winter if subjected to heaters, radiators, and fireplaces.

3. Protect your Yorkie from unsanitary and damp environments that can cause skin problems such as bacterial and fungal infections.

Prevent Skin Allergies

1. Feed your Yorkie a high-quality diet. If he has food allergies, feed him a hypoallergenic diet.

2. Give your Yorkie bedding made of natural materials.

3. Check regularly for parasites, and treat them immediately before they get out of control. Flea allergy dermatitis (FAD) is one of the leading causes of hair loss in dogs.

Skin-Deep Hair Facts

• Healthy skin is absolutely necessary for your Yorkshire Terrier to grow beautiful hair.
• Yorkie hair grows in cycles and sheds throughout the year. Different hairs are in different growth stages.
• Hair is made up of almost solid protein, called keratin. Thirty percent or more of the protein in a Yorkie's diet is used for skin and coat.

• High-quality nutrition improves coat quality more than vitamins, supplements, and hair products.

• Yorkie coats grow about .1 to .2 mm each day. That distance multiplied by the hundreds of thousands of growing hairs on the body totals about 50 feet (150 m) of hair growth each day!

• Hormonal imbalances can cause hair loss or skin problems.

• Photoperiod (the number of hours of light exposure each day) affects Yorkie shedding more than environmental temperature does.

• Daily brushing is necessary to remove dead hairs, stimulate the skin, and distribute natural oils in the coat.

• Your Yorkie's coat mirrors his health status. If he has parasites, allergies, hormonal problems, is sick or fed a poor diet, the problems will be reflected in his coat's poor appearance.

Make Grooming Safe, Easy, and Fun!

1. Designate an area exclusively for grooming, in an easy-to-clean, convenient location close to an electrical outlet (for hair dryer, electric nail file, or vacuum cleaner).

2. Select a table that is high enough for you to work at a comfortable height.

3. Use a nonslip mat or table surface to prevent falls or injury.

4. Start by teaching your Yorkie how to stand and lie down on a grooming table.

5. Teach your Yorkie to allow you to handle his feet so you can trim the feet and nails.

6. Purchase high-quality tools and equipment.

7. Place all the grooming items you need near the grooming table, within easy reach.

8. Use only products designed for use in dogs to ensure a pH balanced for canine skin.

9. *Several short training sessions are better than one long one.*

10. *Never leave your Yorkshire Terrier unattended on the table.*

Grooming Tools and Supplies

Have all supplies handy before you begin:
- Grooming table
- Nonslip mat and towels
- Brush with natural bristle
- Metal double-side comb with wide-spaced and close-spaced teeth
- Rat-tailed comb (from beauty-supply stores) to make partings
- Small hair bands (do not use rubber bands—they cause hair breakage)
- Scissors (blunt tipped)
- Nail trimmers
- Styptic powder or gel
- Spray bottle
- Detangling spray
- Emollient, premium, gentle shampoo (pH balanced for dog skin)
- Gentle hair rinse (for dogs)
- Tissue paper for crackering
- Oil (such as almond oil) for the coat
- Gentle ear-cleaning solution
- Cotton-tipped swabs or cotton balls
- Towels: soft cloth and paper
- Soft washcloths
- Hair dryer
- Electric nail sander (optional)
- Soft toothbrush
- Dog dentifrice (do not use toothpaste for humans)
- Small sink or basin for bathing and rinsing

Crackering

Crackering is a method of wrapping sections of the Yorkie's coat in acid-free tissue paper to protect it and keep it clean and tangle-free. The tissue paper is folded such that a section of hair lies in the center and

then the paper is folded, left and right, over the hair. The paper is then folded in half, and then in half again and secured with a band. The overall appearance is of little square paper "crackers" with a band across the center. Crackering starts with the topknot, then the moustache and chin, and finally the long hairs on the sides of the body.

There are several Yorkie cuts that require less maintenance. You can trim the body hair shorter, so that it doesn't come in contact with the floor. Or, you can clip the top half of the coat, so that only the sides grow long. You can even clip all of the body hair shorter.

Neat Feet!

Trimmed feet look very neat and prevent hair mats, dirt, grass awns, stickers, and excess moisture (leading to bacterial growth, moist dermatitis, and sores) from accumulating between the toes. Trimmed feet also prevent slipping and make walking and running easier.

A beautiful Yorkshire Terrier has the magical power to stop people in their tracks—and then steal their hearts! Yorkies are natural crowd pleasers. Wherever you go with your diminutive darling, he will be the center of attention!

Do not bathe your Yorkie until his coat has been completely combed and detangled!

Step 1—Check skin and hair.

Check the skin for redness, sores, and parasites. Check the hair for mats, knots, and tangles.

Step 2—Wet the coat.

Using a water spray bottle or a coat detangling conditioner, *lightly* wet the coat.

Step 3—"Line brush" the body.

Place your Yorkie on his side, push the hair on the upper side of his body from the chest up over his back. Hold the hair in place with one hand. With the other hand, make a horizontal part and section the bottom portion of the hair in ½ inch (1 cm) increments.

Separate knots and tangles gently, using your fingers. Brush the section of the hair, starting at the skin and ending at the tip of the hairs. Part the coat to isolate another horizontal section of hair above the one you just combed and repeat the process.

Step 4—Brush the fall.

Divide the long hair on your Yorkie's head (fall). Brush and comb the sections.

Step 5—Clean the face.

Use a clean, damp cloth to gently clean away tearing or discharge in the corners of the eyes. Wipe the corners of the nostrils to remove dirt and discharge. Wipe the mouth to remove food particles, hair, and saliva.

Pluck excess hair from the inside of the ears. Clean the inside of the ears with a cotton ball and gentle ear cleaner. Dry the ears. Now put cotton balls in the ears to keep out water during the bath.

Step 6—Bathe your Yorkie.

Adjust the water to a comfortable temperature.

Use a spray hose to saturate the coat with water.

Apply a premium dog shampoo and massage it over the entire body in the direction of hair growth. Start at the center of the back and work downward, to the sides of the body and limbs.

Step 7—Rinse the coat.

Cover your Yorkie's eyes and nose as you rinse. Apply a conditioning rinse throughout the coat, soak, then rinse thoroughly.

Step 8–Dry your Yorkie.

Using soft towels, blot, don't rub, your Yorkie. *Don't let your Yorkie get cold or chilled!*

You can also blow-dry your Yorkie's coat. Dry a small area at a time, blowing in the direction of hair growth. Brush the coat in sections with one hand as you hold the dryer in the other hand.

Do not hold the dryer too close to the skin or you can burn your Yorkie's skin!

Step 9–Make a topknot.

There are several ways to make topknots. You can make a single topknot, on the top center of the head, or a double topknot, with a knot centered above each eye. You can increase the size of the topknot by putting hair gel on the inside hairs and back-brushing them, and then smoothing the top hairs over to cover the knot. Topknots require a lot of practice and patience.

Simple topknot: Part the fall horizontally across the top of the forehead. Start near the outside corners of the eyes, including hair on the forehead behind the eyes. Do not include the hair on the ears. Secure this section of hair with a band and center in on the head. Fold the hair section into a loop at the end so it can be hidden or tucked away with a band, bow, or barrette.

Double topknot: Begin as for a simple single topknot, then divide the hair section vertically into two sections, left and right. Secure each section with a band. Center the left section on the top of the head above the left eye and the right section above the right eye. Fasten each knot with a band, bow, or barrette.

Show topknot: There are different kinds of show topknots. Show topknots consist of two topknots.

Step 10–Trimmings

Carefully shave excess hair from the front and back top one-third to one-half of the ears. Trim excess hair away from the feet with blunt-tipped scissors. Do not trim hair away from the eyes or nose. Lightly trim the moustache. Part the hair down the center of the back, starting at the base of the skull, and trim the coat carefully so it hangs straight and evenly on both sides. Trim excess hair away from the perianal area. Trim the toenails.

Feeding Your Yorkshire Terrier

Your Yorkshire Terrier has special nutritional needs. She has a fast metabolism to fuel. Her diet must be high quality, highly digestible, and energy dense to make every bite count. Feeding your Yorkie a nutritionally complete and balanced diet is one of the most important things you can do to keep her healthy throughout life.

Every aspect of your tiny toy's well-being—from a healthy heart to her beautiful flowing gown—is affected by the quality and quantity of the food she eats. Fortunately, nutrition is one area of your pet's health care over which you have full control.

Your Yorkie has a small stomach, so she must eat frequent small meals. Her stomach is too small to hold enough food in a single meal to supply her daily caloric needs and support her high activity level, especially if she is a young puppy. She must have a good balance of protein, fats, and carbohydrates to prevent hypoglycemia (low blood sugar)—a common problem in Yorkshire Terriers.

LIFE STAGES AND NUTRITION

Nutritional needs change throughout life. As your Yorkie grows, develops, and eventually ages, she needs different diets. For example, a puppy needs a food that provides complete and balanced nutrition for growth and development. When your Yorkie is an adult, she will have greater nutritional needs if she is active, than if she is a sedentary lapdog. Finally, old or sick Yorkies need a diet suited to their health condition, such as a senior diet or a prescription diet.

STARTING OFF RIGHT

When you first bring your Yorkie home, continue feeding her the same diet the breeder was feeding until she has adjusted to her new family and home. A change in diet and feeding schedules during this important adaptation time can be very stressful and cause stomach upset and diarrhea.

Your Yorkie has small teeth, a delicate mouth, and a tiny esophagus. Make sure the food is bite size. Feed your Yorkie food suitable for toy breeds. Don't feed kibble that is too large, too hard, too difficult to eat, or that could cause choking.

Discuss your Yorkie's diet with your veterinarian. If a change in diet is recommended, make the change gradually.

DECIPHERING DOG FOOD LABELS

There are countless brands and types of commercial dog foods available, but not every dog food is good for Yorkshire Terriers. Yorkies need high-quality, energy-rich, highly digestible food.

Dog food comes in all sizes, colors, shapes, and consistencies (dry kibble, semi-moist, moist canned). The brands are packaged and named to attract *you*, the consumer. The challenge is to find a high-quality food that

51

Special Diets

There are prescription diets for several conditions, such as heart failure, kidney failure, urinary problems, and allergies. Consult your veterinarian.

your Yorkie will *eat*. Yorkies can be fussy eaters and difficult to please.

The very best way to select high-quality dog food is to consult with your veterinarian and Yorkshire Terrier breeders. Feed dog food made *from high-quality protein sources*.

You cannot rely entirely on the comparison of ingredient labels to select dog food for your Yorkie. Dog food labels are confusing and do not always tell you what you really need to know.

Ingredients

• Ingredients include *everything* that is mixed together to make the dog food.
• Dog food labels list ingredients in decreasing order of preponderance by weight, but they do not tell you about the ingredients' quality or digestibility.
• Ingredients can be nutritional (protein, carbohydrates, fat, vitamins, minerals) or non-nutritional (food additives, artificial coloring, artificial flavorings, food preservatives).

The list of ingredients tells you nothing about the ingredients' quality or digestibility. Different dog food manufacturers may use the same types of ingredients, but the ingredients can vary in quality.

Nutrients

Nutrients are necessary for life. Some nutrients, such as sugars, amino acids (the building blocks of proteins), and fatty acids, produce energy. Other nutrients may not produce energy, such as water, oxygen, vitamins, and minerals. The type and amount of nutrients contained in a dog food mixture make up the nutrient profile.

Proteins

Protein is the most important health factor in your Yorkie's diet. Protein is needed for muscle, bones, growth, development, immunity against diseases, and to grow that beautiful Yorkie coat.

High-quality animal source proteins are much better for dogs than plant source proteins because they provide a better balance of amino acids and have a high biological value. They are also more digestible and produce less fecal material and gas than plant source proteins. Animal source protein makes up the most expensive part of the diet.

Animal protein sources found in commercial dog foods include beef, chicken, turkey, duck, rabbit, lamb, venison, kangaroo, fish, and eggs. Not all animal source protein is of high nutritional value. Look for the words

Weighing In

A scale is a wise investment. If you weigh your Yorkie once a week and record her weight, you will be able to accurately monitor her growth rate and adjust her diet according to her needs.

Food for Fuel

A high percentage of protein in the diet is not the same as high protein quality. If the diet contains a high percentage of protein, but the protein is of poor quality, your Yorkie will not be able to digest or use much of it.

meat, meal, and *by-products. Meat* means muscle, skin, and organs composed of muscle (heart, diaphragm) and skin, with or without bone. *By-products* include heads, feet, guts, liver, kidneys, brain, spleen, and bone. By-products are less expensive and of poorer-quality protein. *Meal* tells you the protein source is ground into particles (as in "cornmeal"). Meal may contain meat protein plus other tissues, such as organs.

Yorkies cannot live on meat alone. In fact, an all-meat diet is deficient in essential minerals (such as calcium) and other important components necessary for life.

Plant protein sources include soybean meal and soybean oil, and vegetables, such as corn. Corn is cheap, so it makes up a large component of many dog foods. Unfortunately, corn is fattening and also causes allergic skin conditions in many dogs.

Fats

Fats are important components of your Yorkie's daily diet. They add to the flavor of the food, provide energy, and play a major role in digestion and the assimilation of fat-soluble vitamins. The various fats (animal fat, vegetable oils, olive oil, fish oils) each have different effects on the body, and many are used for therapeutic remedies. Omega-3 and omega-6 fatty acids are important ingredients necessary for skin health and hair growth.

Carbohydrates

Carbohydrates are sugars, starches, and fibers. *Researchers have not yet determined the exact amount of carbohydrates required in the canine diet, yet carbohydrates make up the major portion of today's commercial dog foods,* usually in the form of corn, cornmeal, rice, potatoes, wheat, or a combination of grains.

Dogs cannot digest fiber, so it is used in many dog foods to maintain dry matter bulk and for canine weight-reduction diets. High-fiber diets produce greater stool volume than high-protein diets.

Vitamins

Vitamins are classified as fat-soluble: vitamins A, D, E, and K; or water-soluble: all the B vitamins and vitamin C. Dogs make their own vitamin C and do not need supplementation in their diet. Vitamin E plays an important role in skin and coat health.

Vitamins must be correctly balanced in a dog's diet. Vitamin overdose is just as serious as vitamin deficiency. Both cause serious medical problems.

Minerals

Minerals are necessary for skeletal growth and development and muscle and nerve function. Among the minerals required for life are calcium, phosphorus, sodium, potassium, magnesium, zinc, selenium, iron, manganese, copper, and iodine.

Minerals should be provided in a balanced ratio. Excessive mineral supplementation can lead to serious medical conditions.

Additives and Preservatives

Additives and preservatives are substances added to the dog food to improve or enhance color, flavor, and texture, and to extend product shelf life. Additives, such as antioxidants, are added to dog food to help keep fat in the food from becoming rancid over time.

Supplements

If you feed your Yorkie a high-quality dog food, vitamin and mineral supplements are unnecessary, unless prescribed by your veterinarian. By supplementing the diet, you can disrupt the nutritional balance you are striving to provide.

Always consult your veterinarian about any form of supplementation before adding it to your Yorkie's diet.

Homemade Diets

Do not try to formulate your dog's diet. Canine nutrition is a complicated field, and homemade diets usually fall far short of meeting a Yorkie's special nutritional needs.

Raw Diets

Do not feed your Yorkie raw meat, raw chicken, raw eggs, raw fish, or bones (raw or cooked). Your Yorkie can be poisoned by bacterial toxins from *Salmonella* and *E. coli* in raw meat and bones. Because of their tiny size, Yorkies can be more sensitive to these toxins than other animals may be.

FEEDING

Yorkshire Terriers have high caloric needs and a fast metabolism, so ask your veterinarian to help you determine your pet's nutritional needs, and don't rely on dog food label recommendations. No two dogs are alike in their feeding requirements.

The amount you feed your Yorkie depends on the quality of the food you provide and her overall health, activity level, stage of development, and environment.

Wet vs. Dry

Dogs that eat moist, canned diets accumulate plaque and tartar on their teeth faster than dogs that eat dry food.

Most canned foods are expensive and contain more than 70 percent water.

Yorkshire Terrier puppies need several (4–6) small frequent meals throughout the day to prevent hypoglycemia (low blood sugar). Their initial growth phase is during the first six months of life, although technically they are still puppies until 12 months of age. For each meal, make sure the food is available for at least 20 minutes. You may also feed young Yorkies free choice to help prevent hypoglycemia. This means food is

The Right Amount

The best way to know if you are feeding your Yorkie the right food in the right amount is to look at her and feel her. You should be able to feel her ribs, but not see them. The ribs should not feel bony and should have a nice layer of flesh, *not fat*, over them.

Yorkie Feeding Guidelines	
Age	**Feeding Schedule**
Weaning to 8 weeks	Every 3 hours
8 to 12 weeks	Every 4 hours
12 to 24 weeks	Every 5 to 6 hours
6 months and older	Every 6 to 8 hours

available at all times and the puppy can eat whenever she desires.

Always measure the food so you know exactly how much is eaten daily. If you leave food out during the day, be sure to discard old or stale food and replenish the dish with fresh food.

Once-a-day feeding is never enough for a Yorkshire Terrier!

Obesity

Overeating is the most common cause of obesity in dogs. More than one-third of the United States canine population is obese. Obesity is a serious health problem that can lead to heart disease, skeletal and joint problems, and metabolic diseases, such as diabetes. Fortunately, obesity is not as common in Yorkies as it is in other breeds and can be easily prevented.

The most effective way to prevent your Yorkie from becoming overweight is to monitor her food intake, avoid overfeeding, limit snacks and treats, and take her on daily walks.

WATER

Water is the most important of all nutrients. Water is necessary for life because it is needed for digestion, to metabolize energy, and to eliminate waste products from the body. Water makes up more than 70 percent of your Yorkshire Terrier's adult body weight. Dogs lose body water throughout the day, in the urine and feces, and by evaporation, panting, drooling, and foot-pad sweating. Water depletion occurs more rapidly in warm or hot weather or when an animal is active. Body

Water Bottles

Your Yorkie can learn to drink out of a water bottle with a sipper tube. It will keep her facial hair tidier, too. If she drinks from a water bottle, you can easily measure her daily water intake.

Food Allergies

Many dogs develop allergies to corn, cornmeal, corn oil, wheat, and wheat gluten. These allergies often cause serious skin problems and digestive problems. *Your Yorkie may benefit from eating a grain-free diet.*

water must be replaced continually, so your Yorkie must have fresh water available at all times to avoid dehydration.

A 10 percent body water loss can result in death.

If your pet is continually thirsty or drinks more than usual, these could be warning signs for illness, such as diabetes or kidney disease. If she is not drinking enough, she will become dehydrated. If you think your Yorkie is drinking too much, or not drinking enough, contact your veterinarian right away.

FOOD ALLERGIES

Yorkshire Terriers can develop food allergies that cause itchy, reddened skin and hair loss. Hypoallergenic diets have been developed especially for dogs with skin sensitivities and food allergies. They may contain ingredients such as fish, duck, venison, eggs, potatoes, or rice. They do not contain beef, corn, or other foods known to cause skin problems in dogs.

Use stainless steel or ceramic food dishes. Plastic or hard rubber dishes can cause skin allergies and contact dermatitis in some Yorkshire Terriers.

Good Eating Habits

- Do not allow your Yorkie to beg.
- Keep track of your pet's daily food consumption.
- Feed enough to satisfy your Yorkie's nutritional needs.
- Do not feed your Yorkie food intended for humans.
- Feed only healthful treats and use them primarily as training rewards.
- Do not allow others to give treats to your Yorkie without your permission.

Keeping Your Yorkshire Terrier Healthy

The best gift you can give your Yorkshire Terrier is the gift of good health care. A healthy Yorkie is more likely to live a longer, fuller, happier life. In fact, with excellent health care, your little companion may live well into his teens!

The best way to keep your Yorkshire Terrier healthy is to prevent problems before they start. Fortunately, preventive health care is easy. It is also better for your Yorkie, and less expensive for you, to prevent health problems rather than treat them.

Preventive health care includes regular physical examinations, good nutrition, immunizations against disease, an effective parasite control program, daily exercise, regular dental care, and daily grooming.

SELECTING A VETERINARIAN

There are many excellent veterinarians from which to choose. Be as particular about selecting your Yorkie's veterinarians as you are about choosing your own doctor.

Here are some guidelines to help you choose a veterinarian.

1. Find a veterinarian who is knowledgeable about Yorkshire Terriers and their special needs. Ask Yorkshire Terrier breeders, owners, trainers, and groomers whom they would recommend.

2. Make sure the doctors' location, office hours, schedule, and availability fit your schedule and needs. Do the doctors provide care on weekends and holidays? Do they offer evening and emergency services?

3. Meet the doctors and support staff. Are the doctors' assistants *licensed, registered veterinary technicians*?

4. Ask to tour the hospital. Is it clean, organized, and well equipped?

5. Ask about fees for services and types of payment methods available.

Start looking for a veterinarian BEFORE you need one.

YORKIE HEALTH CHECK

A home health check (see Yorkshire Terrier Health Check Sheet) is a good way to detect a possible problem before it becomes serious. *If your Yorkie is not acting normally, is depressed or lethargic, or is not eating and drinking, contact your veterinarian right away.* When illness strikes, your pet's condition can rapidly deteriorate. The sooner his problem is diagnosed and treated, the better his chances are for recovery.

Vaccinations

Vaccinations are the best method currently available to protect against serious, life-threatening diseases. Anywhere you take your Yorkie—parks, rest stops, campgrounds, dog shows, obedience classes, your veterinarian's

Yorkshire Terrier Health Check Sheet

What to Check	Normal Signs	Problems	Possible Causes
Attitude	Alert, happy, outgoing	Depressed, lethargic	Illness, injury
Appearance	Healthy, good body condition, glossy coat	Too thin, too heavy, poor coat condition	Numerous
Eyes	Clear, bright	Discharge	Infection, injury
		Cloudy	Corneal injury, cataracts
		Squinting	Pain, sensitivity to light
		Redness, tearing	Irritation, allergies, trauma, foreign object
Nose	Clean, wet or dry	Discharge	Infection, foreign object in nasal passage
Ears	Clean	Odor, discharge, excessive wax buildup	Parasites, infection, foreign objects
Gums	Bright pink	Pale pink or white	Anemia, parasitism
		Yellow	Jaundice, liver problems
		Blue or gray	Lack of oxygen
		Bright red	Gum disease, heatstroke, poisoning, fever
Teeth	Clean, white	Plaque and tartar, missing teeth	Periodontal disease, dental disease
Posture	Normal	Hunched	Pain
		Neck outstretched or sitting with elbows turned outward	Breathing difficulty
		Drooping head	Neck pain
		Tilted head	Ear pain, infection, ear parasites, foreign object in ear, or nervous system problem
Stance	All feet support weight equally	Limping, favoring a foot, shifting weight	Pain or discomfort from foot to foot
Movement	Walks and runs	Lameness, limping	Pain, injury, trauma, muscular or skeletal or nervous system problems, possible foreign object in foot pad
		Skipping, hopping	Possible patellar luxation (slipped kneecap)
Skin and hair	Clean, healthy skin and glossy coat	Hair loss, sores, dry flaky skin, scratching	Parasites, poor nutrition, injury, hormonal imbalances, inadequate grooming
Under tail	Clean	Swelling, pus, open wound, odor	Anal sac problem, cysts, parasites

American Animal Hospital Association Canine Vaccine Guidelines
(updated 2011)

Core Vaccines (Recommended)	Non-core Vaccines (Optional)	Not Recommended
Canine parvovirus (MLV)	Parainfluenza	Canine coronavirus
Canine distemper (MLV)	*Bordetella*	*Giardia lambia*
Canine adenovirus-2 (MLV)	*Borrelia burgdorferi* (Lyme disease)	
Rabies (killed virus)	*Leptospira*	

*MLV: Modified live virus vaccine

office—he can be exposed to germs that cause severe illness and possibly death. Although there is not a vaccine available for every known canine disease, we do have vaccines for the most common and serious diseases. No vaccine is 100 percent guaranteed effective, but if you are diligent about your pet's health and vaccination schedule, you can rest assured he has a very good chance of being protected against serious contagious illness.

Vaccination is a medical decision, not a calendar event. The type of vaccination, and when it is given, should be determined according to your Yorkie's lifestyle, age, health condition, past medical history, and potential risk of exposure. Vaccination is a potent medical procedure with profound effect. There are significant benefits, as well as some risks, associated with any vaccine.

Guideline Schedule for Core Vaccines for Yorkshire Terrier Puppies

Vaccine	First Inoculation	Second Inoculation	Third Inoculation	First Booster
	Age	Age	Age	Interval
Distemper	8 weeks	12 weeks	16 weeks	1 year
Canine adenovirus-2	8 weeks	12 weeks	16 weeks	1 year
Parvovirus	8 weeks	12 weeks	16 weeks	1 year
Rabies	12 weeks to 16 weeks (state laws vary)			1 year

Common Canine Diseases

Disease	Cause	Spread	Contagion	Symptoms	Treatment
Distemper	Viral	Airborne, body excretions	Highly contagious, especially among young dogs	Respiratory: difficulty breathing, coughing, discharge from nose and eyes Gastrointestinal: vomiting, diarrhea, dehydration Nervous: trembling, blindness, paralysis, seizures Skin: pustules on skin, hard foot pads	Supportive and symptomatic therapy, antibiotics for secondary bacterial infections
Parvovirus	Viral	Contaminated feces	Highly contagious, especially among puppies	Gastrointestinal: diarrhea, dehydration, vomiting Cardiac: heart problems, heart failure	Supportive and symtomatic therapy, antibiotics for secondary bacterial infections
Canine adenovirus (hepatitis)	Viral	Body excretions, urine	Highly contagious, especially among puppies and young dogs	Liver: inflammation, jaundice Eyes: "blue eye" caused by inflammation and fluid buildup Kidney: damage Pain and internal bleeding	Supportive and symtomatic therapy, antibiotics for secondary bacterial infections
Leptospirosis	Bacterial	Urine contaminated in kennels or from wild animals	Highly contagious	Kidney: damage and failure Liver: damage, jaundice Internal bleeding, anemia	Antibiotics and supportive therapy
Parainfluenza *Bordetellosis* Both cause "kennel cough"	Viral Bacterial	Airborne, sneeze and cough droplets	Highly contagious, especially in boarding kennels and at dog shows	Respiratory: dry, hacking, continual cough for several weeks, may cause permanent damage to airways	Supportive therapy plus antibiotics
Coronavirus only	Viral	Feces	Highly contagious	Gastrointestinal symptoms: vomiting, diarrhea, dehydration	Supportive therapy
Lyme disease	Bacterial	Spread by the bite of an infected tick or contaminated body fluids		Swollen lymph nodes, lethargy, loss of appetite, joint swelling, lameness, can induce heart and kidney disease	Supportive therapy plus antibiotics
Rabies	Viral	Saliva (bite wounds)		Fatal, preceded by nervous system signs, including paralysis, incoordination, and change in behavior	None for animals. Post-exposure treatment is available for humans.

Yorkshire Terrier puppies are tiny and sensitive. Just to be safe, your veterinarian may separate the time interval between core vaccines, rather than giving them all at one time.

After the first year's set of booster vaccinations, your veterinarian will advise if subsequent boosters should be once every year, once every two years, or once every three years. Research suggests that vaccinations given once every three years are protective for many dogs. In addition, new vaccines may be available when you consult your veterinarian.

The table suggests guidelines only. Your veterinarian should customize puppy and adult booster vaccinations for your Yorkie based on your dog's health and specific requirements.

Parasite Control

Parasite control has never been easier! We have a wide selection of effective, easy-to-use products that prevent or kill internal (roundworms, hookworms, whipworms, tapeworms, and heartworms) and external (fleas, ticks, and mange-causing mites) parasites. These products are available from your veterinarian and require a physical examination, a heartworm test, and fecal examination, prior to dispensing.

Internal Parasites

Internal parasites (such as worms and protozoa) pose a dangerous threat to your tiny canine's health. They can cause diarrhea and, in severe cases, dehydration, malnutrition, anemia, and death. Take these

Internal Parasites

	Mode of Transmission to Dogs	Mode of Transmission to Humans	Prevention
Roundworms	Ingestion of eggs in feces of infected animals, transmitted from mother to pup *in utero* or in the milk	Accidental ingestion of eggs from contact with infected fecal material	Parasiticides (products that kill parasites)
Hookworms	Ingestion of larvae in feces of infected animals, direct skin contact with larvae	Direct skin contact with larvae in soil contaminated with feces of infected animals, accidental ingestion of larvae	Parasiticides
Whipworms	Contact with feces	None	Parasiticides
Tapeworms	Contact with fleas and feces, ingestion of fleas, eating raw meat (wild rodents)	Accidental ingestion of infected adult flea	Parasiticides
Heartworms	Mosquito bite	None	Parasiticides
Protozoa	Contact with feces	Accidental ingestion of organisms in fecal material	Parasiticides

External Parasites

	Animal Health Problem	Contagious to Humans
Fleas	Allergy to flea saliva, skin irritation and itching, transmission of tapeworms	Fleas may bite humans. Tapeworms also may be indirectly transmitted to people.
Ticks	Transmission of Lyme disease, skin irritation and infection	Humans can contract Lyme disease from direct contact with ticks. Always wear gloves when removing ticks from your dog, to avoid contracting the disease.
Sarcoptic mange	Skin lesions and itching, hair loss	Sarcoptic mange can spread from pets to people by contact.
Demodectic mange	Skin lesions, localized or generalized hair loss	No

internal parasites very seriously. What might be a light parasite load for a bigger breed of dog can be deadly to your Yorkie. Have your veterinarian check your pet regularly for intestinal parasites.

Some canine parasites transmitted through contact with feces are also a health threat to people, especially children. Prevention is simple: good hygiene, a clean environment, and reminding children to wash their hands after handling animals and before eating.

Illness

Your Yorkshire Terrier may act tough, but if he gets sick, his health can take a nosedive very quickly. If your Yorkie is not feeling well, do not waste a moment. Contact your veterinarian right away. Early treatment makes all the difference between rapid recovery and prolonged illness, or even death, for a little Yorkie.

Contact your veterinarian right away if your Yorkie has any of the following problems:

- Fever
- Pain
- Loss of appetite
- Lethargy
- Vomiting
- Diarrhea
- Coughing
- Sneezing
- Wheezing
- Difficulty breathing
- Difficulty swallowing
- Choking
- Limping
- Head shaking
- Trembling
- Blood in the urine or stools
- Inability to urinate or defecate
- Severe constipation
- Dehydration
- Weight loss
- Signs of nervous system problems (such as seizures or paralysis)

FIRST AID FOR YOUR YORKSHIRE TERRIER

Be prepared for an emergency. Put all your supplies together so you will have them on hand when you need them and won't waste precious time during an emergency trying to find them.

Make a copy of the emergency instructions in this book and put it in your Yorkie's first aid kit so you can refer to it easily. Keep your veterinarian's daytime and emergency telephone numbers, and the poison control

> **For ALL medical conditions and emergencies, contact your veterinarian immediately.**

telephone number, in the first aid kit. When you travel with your Yorkie, take his first aid kit with you.

Supplies for Your First Aid Kit

Basic supplies and materials for your Yorkie's first aid kit can be purchased at your local pharmacy or from your veterinarian.

First aid kit supplies:
- ✔ Bandage scissors
- ✔ Small, regular, blunt-tipped scissors
- ✔ Thermometer
- ✔ Tourniquet
- ✔ Tweezers
- ✔ Syringes (12 cc with curved plastic tips are good to flush wounds)
- ✔ Mouth gag (or small wooden dowel)
- ✔ Hydrogen peroxide 3 percent solution
- ✔ Triple antibiotic ointment (bacitracin, neomycin, polymyxin)
- ✔ Roll of gauze bandage
- ✔ Gauze pads
- ✔ Telfa no-stick pads
- ✔ Sterile dressing and compresses
- ✔ Sterile saline solution
- ✔ Elastic bandage (preferably waterproof)
- ✔ Self-adhesive bandage (Vet Wrap type)
- ✔ Activated charcoal (for treatment of poisoning)
- ✔ Eyewash
- ✔ Antihistamines (diphenhydramine or chlorpheneramine)
- ✔ Ophthalmic ointment
- ✔ Cold compress
- ✔ Muzzle (gauze strip will work)
- ✔ Blanket
- ✔ Paper towels
- ✔ Soap
- ✔ Sponge
- ✔ Exam gloves (vinyl)
- ✔ Penlight
- ✔ Flashlight
- ✔ Bottled water
- ✔ Pedialyte
- ✔ Nutrical (or other high-sugar product such as Karo syrup)
- ✔ Plastic bags
- ✔ Clippers (optional, but handy to shave wound areas)

The goal of first aid treatment is to give your Yorkie whatever emergency care he needs to save his life or reduce pain and suffering until you can contact your veterinarian. *Always muzzle your dog before initiating emergency treatment, for the safety of your pet and everyone involved.* Your Yorkie may behave unpredictably when he is in pain or frightened. He may instinctively snap out in self-defense and bite you.

If someone else is available, save time by having the person contact your veterinarian for advice while you begin emergency treatment.

Yorkie ABCs: Airway, Breathing, Circulation

The most important things to check first in an emergency are the following:

1. Is the airway (trachea) unobstructed and open?

2. Is your pet breathing?

3. Is the heart beating?

- **Airway.** Your Yorkie has a tiny throat and very tiny trachea (windpipe). If his airway is obstructed, he can quickly suffocate. Removing foreign objects from a Yorkie's throat is difficult. Carefully open the mouth to see what is blocking the air passageway. Yorkies have delicate jaws, so be very gentle. Use a small gag to keep the mouth open so you are not bitten. Use a flashlight or penlight to look down the throat to find the obstruction. Be very careful not to push the object farther down the throat with your fingers. Forceps may be necessary to retrieve the object.
- **Breathing.** If your Yorkie is not breathing, you must act quickly and breathe for him, or he will suffocate. Open his mouth, and remove any objects, debris, or saliva. Gently pull his tongue out straight so it does not block the throat. Place your mouth over his nose and muzzle. Make a tight seal. Blow a breath gently into the nostrils and watch for the chest to rise. Then stop, so air can be expelled. Repeat this procedure, blowing a breath every 5 to 10 seconds, as you are able, until your Yorkie breathes without your help. Be very careful. Your Yorkie's tiny lungs do not have much capacity. Do not blow too hard or you can overinflate and damage his tiny lungs. Check gum color often. The gums should return to a bright pink color if your Yorkie is receiving enough oxygen.

Note: Be careful! Do this procedure only if your Yorkie is unconscious or you can be bitten!

- **Cardiac.** If you cannot hear a heartbeat, or feel a pulse, begin cardiopulmonary resuscitation (CPR) immediately. Lay your pet on his right side. Place your hands on top of

each other and gently press your fingers on the left side of the chest, slightly above and directly behind the elbow. Continue to press and release at a rate of one to two presses every second. Remember to also breathe into the nostrils every 5 to 10 seconds, as you are able. Continue CPR until your pet is able to breathe on his own and you can feel a pulse.

Anal Sacs

Dogs have two anal sacs, one on each side of the rectum. The sacs contain a strong-smelling brown liquid. Anal sacs normally empty during defecation because of pressure against the sacs. Sometimes anal sacs fail to empty, the brown liquid thickens or turns to a thick paste consistency, and

the sacs enlarge and need to be emptied manually by a veterinarian. If the anal sacs are plugged or impacted, they become irritated and painful. If left untreated, they may become infected or rupture, in which case they require immediate veterinary treatment. Anal sac problems are common in Yorkies.

Bite Wounds

The most common wounds Yorkies suffer are bite wounds. When Yorkies suffer dog attacks, the injuries are usually severe. Wounds to the head, neck, chest, and abdomen can be very serious. Wounds that penetrate the body cavity are life threatening, especially if the lungs are partially collapsed or the internal organs are exposed. Immediate emergency veterinary care is needed.

If body organs are protruding from an abdominal wound, cover them gently with a warm, sterile, damp saline dressing. Do not push the organs back into the body. Rush your Yorkie to the hospital.

Consult your veterinarian immediately about any bite-wound injuries, antibiotics, and possible surgical repair. If a stray or a wild animal (such as a raccoon or coyote) has bitten your Yorkie, discuss the possible risk of rabies with your veterinarian.

Bleeding

Bleeding or hemorrhage occurs from injury, trauma, or serious health problems. Use a gauze or clean towel as a compress to apply firm pressure over the wound to stop the bleeding. If a large blood vessel in a limb has been severed, hemorrhage is life threatening. Keep pressure on the area and rush your Yorkie to your veterinarian or an emergency clinic.

Bone Fractures

Fractures are among the most common injuries Yorkshire Terriers suffer. Many fractures are caused by owners accidentally stepping on their Yorkies, being dropped by children, falling off furniture, or being roughed up by larger dogs.

Signs of bone fractures include swelling, pain and tenderness, abnormal limb position or movement, limping, and crepitation.

Yorkie bones are tiny, and it is difficult to make splints for them. Keep your pet as comfortable as you can, place him on a soft bed, keep him calm and warm, and restrict his activity. Take him to your veterinarian immediately.

Burns

Your Yorkshire Terrier can suffer three kinds of burns:

Thermal burns—from fire, boiling liquids, appliances

Electrical burns—from chewing on electrical cords

Chemical burns—from a variety of chemicals (such as corrosives, oxidizing agents, desiccants, and poisons)

If your Yorkie is burned, immediately cool the burn by applying a cold, wet cloth or an ice pack to the area. Protect the burned area from the air with an ointment (Neosporin or aloe vera). If he has suffered a chemical burn, immediately flush the burn profusely with water or saline to dilute and rinse the caustic chemical from the area. Do not let your Yorkie lick the area or he will burn his mouth and esophagus with the caustic substance. Contact your veterinarian immediately.

Choking

Choking is treated as previously described in Yorkie ABCs.

Cuts

Cuts should be cleaned well and treated with antibiotics to prevent infection. Serious cuts may require sutures, so contact your veterinarian for advice. If the cut is not too deep, wash it with a mild soap and rinse it several times with water. Dry the wound well and apply an antibiotic ointment to it. If the cut is in an area that can be bandaged, wrap the area with gauze and elastic bandage to prevent contamination and infection. *Do not wrap the bandage too tightly. Change the bandage daily.* Consult your veterinarian.

Dehydration

Dehydration means the body has lost too much water. The most common causes of dehydration in Yorkies are vomiting, diarrhea, and heat exposure. A dehydrated Yorkie has also lost important minerals from the body.

Treatment for dehydration is the replenishment of fluids. If your pet is conscious, offer him water to drink. Do not force water down his throat if he is unconscious or too weak to drink on his own. Doing so can cause him to aspirate water into his lungs. Keep a bottle of Pedialyte on hand for emergencies. Contact your veterinarian immediately.

Heatstroke

Heatstroke is caused by exposure to high temperature. Confinement in a car is one of the leading causes of heatstroke. On a hot day, a car parked in the shade, with the

69

windows partially open, can reach temperatures exceeding 120°F (48.9°C) within a few minutes. Overexertion on a hot day can also cause heatstroke. Dogs that are old or overweight are especially prone to heatstroke.

Signs of heatstroke include rapid breathing, panting, bright red gums, thick saliva, vomiting, diarrhea, dehydration, and a rectal temperature of 105 to 110°F (41–43°C). As the condition progresses, the animal weakens, goes into shock, becomes comatose, and dies. Heatstroke can kill a Yorkie in a few short minutes.

If your Yorkie is suffering from heatstroke, you must lower his body temperature immediately, but not too quickly. A rapid temperature drop can cause more problems. Cool your pet by repeatedly wetting him down with cool (not cold!) water.

Check his body temperature every three minutes. When the temperature has dropped to 102°F (39°C), stop wetting with cool water and monitor your pet closely. When he is conscious, offer him water to drink.

Heatstroke is a medical emergency that requires immediate veterinary care. Intravenous fluids and various medications to treat shock and prevent cerebral edema (brain swelling) are necessary to ensure survival. Contact your veterinarian immediately.

Hypoglycemia

Hypoglycemia (low blood sugar) is a common cause of death in Yorkshire Terriers. Yorkies are active and burn a lot of calories, so they need to be fed several times throughout the day (as often as every three to eight hours, depending on age and activity level).

Symptoms of hypoglycemia are drowsiness, lethargy, inactivity, weakness, and nervous system signs such as lack of coordination. If not treated immediately, seizures and death quickly follow.

Do not force food or liquid into your Yorkie's mouth if he is unconscious. He can aspirate and choke to death. Instead, rub a sugar-rich substance on the gums, such as Nutrical (available from your veterinarian) or Karo syrup (corn syrup). Hypoglycemia is often accompanied by hypothermia and dehydration. Wrap your pet in a blanket, keep him warm, and rush him to your veterinarian.

Hypothermia

Yorkshire Terriers are tiny, and most do not have much body fat. Do not let all that hair fool you, either. The silky coat does not give enough insulation or protection from the cold. Very young Yorkies are fragile and are especially sensitive to the cold. Once they start to lose body heat, they cannot regain it without help. Signs of hypothermia begin with shivering and progress to lethargy, slow heart rate, slow respiration, coma, and death.

Warm your Yorkie *slowly*! Rapid heating, or overheating, causes serious problems. Warm your pet by covering him with a blanket. Leave his head exposed so you can watch him closely, and place him in a warm area. *Do not use an electric heating pad.* Instead, fill plastic water bottles with very warm (not hot!) water and wrap them in towels. Place the water bottles near, but not directly against, his body. Refill the bottles when they are no longer warm enough. Check your Yorkie's body temperature (rectally) every five minutes until it has returned to normal. Do not allow his temperature to rise above 101.5°F (39°C). Observe your pet closely for signs of problems. Follow-up care is necessary, so contact your veterinarian right away.

Eye Injury

Eye injuries are extremely painful. Serious injuries can result in loss of vision, or even loss of the eyes. Injured eyes can be very sensitive to light. If your Yorkie has an eye problem, put him in an area with subdued lighting. Contact your veterinarian immediately. If rinsing is needed, use a commercial eyewash solution or ophthalmic saline solution. When you transport your pet to the hospital, cover the travel kennel with a towel to help keep out as much light as possible.

Insect Stings

Most insect stings occur on the face, front legs, and feet. A severe allergic reaction can lead to facial and throat swelling, making it difficult or impossible to breathe. In extreme cases, anaphylactic shock and death can result.

Bees leave their stingers in the skin, but wasps and hornets do not. If a bee stings your Yorkie, you can remove the stinger by scraping it gently in one direction with a stiff business card. If that does not work, remove the stinger with tweezers. Be gentle and try not to squeeze the stinger, or more venom will be injected into the site. Apply a paste mixture of water and baking soda or an ice pack to the stung area to relieve pain. If the offending insect is a hornet or wasp, apply vinegar to the area for pain relief. Later, you may also put a topical antihistamine cream around the sting site. Sensitive animals often benefit from antihistamines such as diphenhydramine (Benadryl) or chlorpheneramine.

Watch your pet closely for the next two hours for signs of illness. If the swelling worsens, or if your Yorkie has difficulty breathing, starts to vomit, develops diarrhea, or loses consciousness, contact your veterinarian immediately. This is a life-threatening situation, and immediate emergency treatment is necessary.

Poisoning

Poisoning is caused by eating, or inhaling toxic substances, or by contact with poisons on the skin, mucous membranes, or eyes.

Signs of poisoning include restlessness, drooling, abdominal pain, vomiting, diarrhea, unconsciousness, seizures, shock, and death.

Many dogs are poisoned by foods and medications intended for their owners. When left alone, a curious Yorkie might explore inside a purse, on top of the coffee table, or on the floor, where food or medicine may have accidentally fallen.

As more new foods and drugs appear on the market, there is an increased risk for potential animal poisoning. For example, xylitol, an artificial sweetener found in baked goods and sugar-free gums, is highly toxic to dogs. Mirabegon, a drug for overactive bladder in people, has recently been found to be highly toxic for dogs. Both of these products cause signs of poisoning rapidly, leaving little time to rush to an emergency clinic for life-saving treatment.

Common Poisonings in Dogs
- Ibuprofen (Advil, Motrin)
- Chocolate
- Ant and roach baits
- Rodenticides (rat, mouse, gopher bait)
- Acetaminophen (Tylenol)
- Pseudoephedrine in cold medicines (Pseudofed)
- Thyroid hormones (overdose)
- Bleach
- Fertilizer
- Hydrocarbons (found in paint, varnish, engine cleaners, furniture polish, lighter fluid)

If your Yorkie has been exposed to poison, contact your veterinarian immediately. If the poison came in a container, read the container label and follow the emergency instructions for treating the poisoning. If the instructions tell you to induce vomiting, you can do this by giving ½ teaspoon of hydrogen peroxide 3 percent.

Activated charcoal can be used to dilute and adsorb ingested poisons. You can buy activated charcoal in liquid, powder, or tablet form from your veterinarian to keep in your first aid kit. If you do not have activated charcoal, you can dilute poison in the gastrointestinal tract by giving milk. Rush your Yorkie to an emergency hospital.

Seizures

There are many causes of seizures, including trauma and poisoning. Epileptic seizures

are common in Yorkshire Terriers. Epilepsy can be hereditary (genetic), or idiopathic (meaning the cause is unknown), or it can be triggered by other health problems.

Seizures may be mild or severe, ranging from a mild tremor of short duration, to violent convulsions, chomping jaws and frothing at the mouth, stiffening of the neck and limbs, and cessation of breathing. During a severe seizure, an animal is not conscious and can be hurt thrashing about on the floor. Your Yorkie may seem to be choking during a seizure, but avoid handling his mouth, or you will be bitten.

Try to prevent your pet from injuring himself during the seizure. After a seizure, your Yorkie will be exhausted and seem dazed.

Place him in a quiet room with subdued light. Keep him comfortable and warm. When he is conscious, offer him some water. Contact your veterinarian immediately for follow-up medical care and to determine the cause of the seizure and how to possibly prevent another one from occurring.

Shock

Shock is a serious emergency condition in which there is a decreased blood supply to vital organs and the body tissues die. Blood loss, heatstroke, bacterial toxins, and severe allergic reactions can all cause shock.

Shock results in a rapid death unless immediate veterinary care—including fluid and oxygen therapy and necessary medications—

are provided. Signs of shock include vomiting, diarrhea, weakness, difficulty breathing, increased heart rate, collapse, and coma.

Snakes, Toads, Scorpions, and Spiders

Your Yorkie is a digger and an explorer. This means he can encounter danger anywhere—in the backyard, or in the great outdoors during a hike, or on a camping trip.

Poisonous snakebites. Common symptoms of snakebite include immediate severe pain, swelling, darkened tissue coloration, and tissue necrosis (tissue death).

Urgent, immediate veterinary attention is necessary. If the bite is left untreated, the skin and underlying tissue may slough off (rot). The amount of venom injected (envenomization) cannot be determined simply by the appearance of the bite wound, but because Yorkies are so tiny, it takes only a small amount of venom to kill them. Signs of snakebite poisoning include weakness, neurological signs, respiratory depression, and shock. Without treatment, death can follow.

Toad poisoning. Poisonous toads in the United States include the Colorado Rim Toad and the Marine Toad. The most toxic toad varieties are in the southwestern desert, the southeastern United States, and Hawaii. If your Yorkie has come in contact with a poisonous toad, contact your veterinarian immediately.

Spiders and scorpions. The brown spiders (fiddleback, brown recluse, and Arizona brown spider) are found in the southern United States. There is no antidote available for their venomous bites. Black widow spiders are found throughout the United States. There is an antivenin available for black widow bites. Scorpions may be found in the southwest United States. Consult your veterinarian right away.

THE SENIOR YORKSHIRE TERRIER

A Yorkshire Terrier is considered a senior citizen when he reaches seven years of age, although for many Yorkies that just might be the halfway mark in their lives. As your Yorkie ages, you may notice changes in his behavior, activity level, and physical stature. He may slow down, sleep more, or have problems with urination or defecation. Yorkies develop plaque and periodontal disease faster than many breeds, especially in their old age. Your Yorkie's hair coat may become thinner, the skin less supple, and warts and other skin growths may appear. Cataracts become visible, hearing

may diminish, and your little friend will rely more on his sense of smell. Muscle weakening, arthritis, a reduction in organ function (heart, liver, kidneys), decreased resistance to disease, and even senility may occur. These are all signs of the aging process.

Here's how to keep your pet comfortable in his golden years.

✔ Keep your Yorkie comfortable and warm.

✔ Provide a soft, warm bed.

✔ Take your Yorkie out daily for slow, easy, short walks on level, soft, nonslippery surfaces, and keep his toenails trimmed.

✔ Do not let your Yorkie try to jump on or off furniture or climb stairs.

✔ Carry your Yorkie when he is tired.

✔ Feed a diet appropriate for your pet's age, health condition, and activity level.

✔ Schedule physical examinations for your senior Yorkie every six months so you can detect any age-related problems early.

✔ If your Yorkie's eyesight is failing, or he is hard of hearing, try not to startle him. Speak to him reassuringly as you approach so he knows you are there.

Euthanasia

Even with the best care in the world, the sad day will come when you must consider euthanasia for your beloved companion. Euthanasia means putting an animal to death humanely, peacefully, and painlessly.

The decision of when to euthanize depends on many things. A good guideline is that if your little companion is suffering and the suffering cannot be relieved, or if the quality of life is so poor that the bad days outnumber the good days, then it is time to discuss

euthanasia with your veterinarian. Your veterinarian can answer questions you have and also help you if you wish to find a pet cemetery or desire cremation services.

During this time, take comfort in the knowledge that you pampered your precious friend throughout his life and that you always made the best decisions regarding his health and welfare—even when you had to make the most difficult decision of all.

SELECTED MEDICAL CONDITIONS

Every dog breed is predisposed to certain health problems. Here are some medical conditions seen more often in Yorkies, although many other breeds also share these health problems. If you purchased your pet from a reputable breeder, it is likely that he will not have any of these conditions, but if he does, the following will help you recognize the problem at the onset.

Dental
• Overcrowded teeth, missing teeth, retained baby (deciduous) teeth, periodontal and gum disease, hairs trapped between teeth. Bad breath, inflammation, sore mouth, reluctance to eat.

Eyes
• **Corneal dystrophy.** Opacity of the cornea, usually resolves in a few months, without treatment, in Yorkie puppies.

- **Dry eye (keratoconjunctivitis sicca, KCS).** Abnormality of the composition of tear film, leading to eye discomfort and visual impairment, can be caused by autoimmune problems.
- **Entropion.** Rolling inward of the eyelid margin toward the globe of the eye. Eyelashes and tissue rub on the cornea, causing irritation and sometimes ulceration.
- **Juvenile cataracts.** Opacity of the lenses, vision impairment, or blindness. Hereditary.
- **Lacrimal (tear) duct problems.** Plugged tear ducts prevent tearing, causing dry, irritated eyes. Treatment: Your veterinarian can flush the tear ducts open to restore normal tearing.
- **Progressive retinal atrophy.** A degenerative disease of the cells of the retina, leading to blindness. Hereditary.

Skin

- **Short hair syndrome.** The long, silky hairs fail to achieve full length, or are shed before reaching normal length. Believed to be caused by a shortened hair cycle. Onset at one to five years of age. No treatment available.

Respiratory

- **Tracheal collapse.** Flattening of the tracheal rings causing a reduction in the diameter of the trachea. May be congenital. Suggested causes include cartilage defect. Signs are observed at an early age and usually follow activity, play, or excitement. If the collapse is in the cervical area, there is coughing and respiratory obstruction on inspiration (inhaling). If the collapse is intrathoracic (in the chest area), the signs are more severe during expiration (exhaling) or cough. Both types of collapse can occur separately or simultaneously. A characteristic "goose honk" cough is frequently noted. Retching and fainting can also occur. Treatment depends on each individual case and consists of rest, reducing stress, possible surgery, a wide selection of medications (corticosteroids, antibiotics, bronchodilators), and weight reduction if needed. Tracheal collapse is common in Yorkies.

Circulatory

- **Patent ductus arteriosis (PDA).** An opening between the aorta and pulmonary artery that fails to close after birth. PDA is common in Yorkies and is genetically inherited. PDA leads to left-sided congestive heart failure. Signs of PDA include a continuous heart murmur ("machinery murmur"), shortness of breath, and coughing. Females are more often affected than males. Treatment is surgical closure of the opening.
- **Portosystemic liver shunt (PSS).** PSS is a congenital problem in which there is an abnormal communication between the portal and systemic circulation. Yorkies are predisposed to liver PSS. The liver removes many toxins, including ammonia, from the blood. In liver PSS, blood that would normally flow through the liver is instead diverted and flows directly into the circulation, and toxins are not removed. Toxins build up in the body, causing encephalopathy and nervous system problems, liver damage, stunted growth, personality changes, depression, seizures, coma, and blindness. Signs of PSS are usually apparent early in life. When possible, PSS is corrected surgically by finding and tying

The Basics: Vital Signs

• **Heart rate:** You can take your Yorkie's heart rate in two ways:

1. Place your fingers between your dog's ribs on the left side of the chest, behind the elbow, and feel the heartbeat.

2. Place your fingers on the inside middle portion of either upper thigh. You can also place your finger in the groin area. Count the number of pulses you feel in a minute. *Normal resting pulse is 80 to 130 beats per minute, depending on age and whether the animal is at rest or has just been very active.*

• **Temperature:** Take your Yorkie's temperature rectally. A digital thermometer is recommended. (Ear thermometers designed for animal use are available from your veterinarian or local pet store. They may be less accurate.) Lubricate the tip of the rectal thermometer and gently insert it a distance of about 1 inch (2.5 cm) into your Yorkie's rectum. Support your dog so he does not sit on the thermometer, and try to keep him calm.

Normal Yorkie body temperature is 101.5 to 102°F (39°C).

• **Circulation:** Capillary refill time (CRT) is a good indicator of circulation. Press on the gums for a second with your finger. The gums should return to a bright pink color as the capillaries refill. *Normal CRT is two seconds or less.*

• **Respiration rate:** Count how many breaths your Yorkie takes in one minute. Respiration rate increases with excitement, heat, or difficulty breathing.

Normal respiration is 15 to 30 breaths per minute.

off the shunt(s) to prevent liver failure and death. If surgery is not possible, the condition can sometimes be managed by a strict high-protein diet and medications.

Nervous System

• **Epilepsy.** Seizures.

• **Hydrocephalus.** Hydrocephalus is caused by cerebrospinal fluid buildup in the ventricles (spaces) of the brain, resulting in compression and brain damage. Signs include a domed head with wide-set eyes, open fontanelles, seizures, visual problems, abnormal eye movements, and learning impairment.

Symptoms vary according to severity. Hydrocephalus is apparent at birth or by several months of age. Treatment is difficult, expensive, and not always successful.

• **Steroid responsive tremor syndrome (also known as little white shaker dog syndrome).** Nervous system disorder (first diagnosed in small, white dogs) that begins with head and body tremors that worsen with exercise or stress. The cause has not been identified but is thought to be linked to an autoimmune and neurotransmitter problem. Affected dogs respond well to treatment with immunosuppressive corticosteroids.

Skeletal

- **Atlantoaxial subluxation.** The second cervical vertebra (bone in the neck) flexes dorsally, causing compression of the spinal cord and serious neurological deficits. Usually caused by abnormal development or degeneration of the atlantoaxial joint. Most common in Yorkies less than one year of age. Thought to be hereditary in Yorkies but also caused by trauma. Causes abnormal gait, neck pain, and death from respiratory paralysis in severe cases.
- **Elbow luxation.** Usually present at birth in some Yorkies because of failure to correctly form intra-articular ligaments during embryonic development. Limb deformities ranging from mild subluxation of the head of the radius, to severe bowing of the foreleg, to inability to extend the forelimb. Signs include inability to bear weight on the affected limb, pain, lameness, and abnormal gait.
- **Hemivertebra.** Abnormal development of the spinal vertebrae causing them to be wedge-shaped. Diagnosed by X-rays. Some Yorkies show no obvious problems. Others may have hind leg weakness, spinal curvature, or pain in the spine.
- **Legg-Calvé-Perthes Disease.** Necrosis (tissue death) of the head of the femur (part of the leg bone that fits into the hip socket) resulting in hind limb lameness in Yorkies between 4 and 11 months of age, pain, limited motion, and shrinkage of thigh muscles.
- **Open fontanelles.** "Soft spots" on the skull caused by failure of bones in the skull to close.
- **Patellar luxation (slipped kneecaps).** A hereditary abnormality of the entire hind

limb, in which the patella (kneecap) slips out of place, causing the lower rear leg to "lock" and produce a skipping or hopping gait until the knee slips back into its groove. The condition occurs at a young age, tends to worsen with growth and age, and may need to be corrected surgically to prevent pain, lameness, and degenerative joint disease.
- **Cryptorchidism.** One or both testicles retained in the abdominal cavity. Treatment: surgical removal. If the testicle(s) is not removed from the abdominal cavity, it can become cancerous (Sertoli cell tumor).

The Talented Yorkshire Terrier

Yorkshire Terriers are more than beautiful charmers. They are animated, intelligent, and competitive. Yorkies are showoffs. They sparkle in the ring. They are always in the spotlight, and they love being the center of attention. No wonder Yorkies always steal the show! So, let's take a look at some of the fun ways you can put your Yorkie's talents to the test.

THE VERSATILE YORKIE: CANINE GOOD CITIZEN

Yorkies that participate in conformation and sports have to be obedient and well mannered, too. So why not get credit for good behavior? The American Kennel Club offers a Canine Good Citizenship award for dogs that can prove they have social etiquette. Some of the requirements for a Canine Good Citizenship award include politely interacting with a stranger (allow being petted and examined, remain with a stranger while you leave briefly); walking on a leash without pulling; obeying the *sit, down, stay,* and *come* commands; and behaving well around other dogs and people.

COMPETITIVE EVENTS

Dog shows are a lot of fun for both exhibitors and observers. Dogs are judged on how closely they meet the ideal standard for conformation for their breeds. If your Yorkie is handsome enough to compete against the best of his breed, join the American Yorkshire Terrier Club and a local kennel club. These clubs will give you information on show dates and locations, judges, professional handlers, canine sports, and other activities. Clubs offer handling classes to teach you and your canine the rules of the games and how to participate in events. Dog clubs also organize fun matches—dog shows where you can practice and perfect what you've learned before taking the big leap into a real all-breed or specialty show.

Fun Matches

Fun matches are just that—*fun*! They are hosted by American Kennel Club–approved breed clubs and conducted according to American Kennel Club show rules. Only

terrier haughty arrogance is expected! Fun matches are a great way to meet other Yorkie exhibitors and learn from them. You can practice all aspects of a real dog show, from traveling to grooming to exhibiting.

Conformation

When your Yorkie looks his very best and you both are fully prepared, you can enter the competitive world of conformation. Be sure to pack everything you need in advance, get lots of rest, and remember it's all about showing off your Yorkie and having fun. The winner of the day depends on the judge, handling skill, and quality of the dogs in the ring on that given day. If you don't win today, don't be discouraged. Only one dog walks away with the top prize at a show. Next time it might be yours!

Under the American Kennel Club show regulations, there are two types of conformation shows: specialty shows and all-breed shows. Dogs are judged according to their breed standard, and by a process of elimination, one dog is selected as best of breed.

• A specialty show is limited to a designated breed. The show is held under AKC rules and sponsored by individual breed clubs. Each year the Yorkshire Terrier Club of America holds an annual national specialty show.

• All-breed shows

All-breed shows are for *all* breeds. Judging is conducted according to AKC rules. In addition to best-of-breed winners, open shows offer the title of best in group (for dogs considered to be the best representative of their group) and best in show (for the dog selected as the best representative of its breed and

purebred, AKC-registered dogs may participate. Fun matches do not count toward points for a championship, and dogs that have won points toward a championship do not compete. Judges at fun matches may be official AKC judges or a knowledgeable dog breeder or handler selected by the hosting club. You can prepare yourself and your puppy for a future in the conformation ring by attending fun matches. They can help you get over the jitters if you are nervous about showing, because in a big competition, you must handle your dog with confidence. Your Yorkie has to have more than a happy, outgoing personality for the show ring. He has to sparkle and radiate self-assurance. A dash of

group, compared with all other dogs of other breeds and groups).

Most dogs competing in specialty or open shows are competing for points toward their championship. A dog can earn from one to five points at a show. The number of points available depends upon the number of entries. Wins of three, four, or five points are called majors.

To become a champion, a Yorkshire Terrier must win a minimum of 15 points by competing in formal, American Kennel Club–sanctioned, licensed events. The points must be won under at least three different judges as follows: two majors won under two different judges, with one or more of the balance of points being won under a judge or judges who did not award the first two majors.

There are five different classes in which a Yorkie can compete for championship points, and the classes are divided by sex:
- Puppy class (divided into 6–9 months of age and 9–12 months of age)
- Novice
- Bred by exhibitor
- American bred
- Open

Male dogs are judged first in this order: puppy dogs, novice dogs, bred-by-exhibitor dogs, American-bred dogs, and open dogs. The first-place winners in each class return to the show ring to compete against one another in the winners class. The dog selected as the best male in the winners class is the winners dog. This is the dog that will win the championship points in the show. The male that placed second to the winners dog in his original class (that is, puppy, novice, bred by exhibitor, American bred, or open) is then brought in to join the winners class and compete against the remaining four dogs in the class. The dog that wins second place in the winners class is the reserve winners dog. If, for any reason, the AKC disallows the championship points to the winners dog, the reserve winners dog will receive the points. The same procedure is then followed, in the same order, for the females, and the winners bitch (who also wins championship points) and reserve winners bitch are selected.

The winners dog and winners bitch then join a class called the best of breed. In this class are entered dogs and bitches that have already won their championship titles. The judge selects either the winners dog or the winners bitch to be best of winners and finishes the judging by selecting from the group an animal to be best of breed. If the best-of-

breed winner is a male, the judge selects the best bitch to be best of opposite sex to the best of winners. If the best-of-breed winner is a female, the judge selects a male for best of opposite sex to the best of winners.

At an all-breed show, judging takes place for each breed, and then each best-of-breed winner competes in its breed group.

The first-place winners of each breed group then compete against each other for the coveted title of best in show.

Grand Championship

A championship title is hard to earn and is only awarded to the very best of the best in conformation. It takes hard work, diligence, patience, and dedication to win enough points for the highly coveted title of Champion. But the competition doesn't stop there! If your Yorkie is spectacular in every way, he can become a Grand Champion!

To earn a Grand Champion title, the dog must first already be a Champion. The dog must earn a total of 25 points with three major wins (a major is worth three points or higher, depending on the number of dogs competing). The major wins must be obtained under three different judges, and at least one other judge must award the remaining points. In other words, your dog must be exhibited— and win—under at least four different judges to become a Grand Champion.

Obedience Trials

In these competitions, it's intelligence that counts, so count Yorkies in!

Dogs are put through a series of exercises and commands and judged according to how well they perform. Each dog starts out with 200 points. Points are deducted throughout the trials for lack of attention, nonperformance, barking, or slowness.

Obedience trials are divided into three levels increasing in difficulty: Novice—Companion Dog (C.D.), Open—Companion Dog Excellent (C.D.X.), and Utility—Utility Dog (U.D.).

To earn a C.D. title, the dog must be able to perform six exercises: heel on leash, stand for examination, heel free, recall, long sit, and long down. To earn a C.D.X. title the dog must be able to heel free, drop on recall, retrieve on flat, retrieve over the high jump, broad jump, long sit, and long down. To earn a U.D., the dog must be able to respond to signal exercise, scent discrimination tests, directed retrieve, directed jumping, and group examination. The dog must earn three legs to earn its title. To receive a leg the dog must earn at least 170 points out of a possible perfect score of 200 and receive more than 50 percent on each exercise.

Agility Competitions

Agility competitions are lots of fun and very exciting. They suit many Yorkies perfectly because they are fast paced and challenging. Agility is performed *off* lead, so before your Yorkie can participate in these competitions, he must obey basic commands very well.

In agility, dogs compete off lead in obstacle courses, jump over objects, teeter on seesaws, cross bridges, run through tunnels, jump through hoops, and weave through poles. These activities complement a Yorkie's

natural abilities and instinctive behaviors. The jumps and obstacles are adjusted to the size of the dog, and the events are timed.

Many titles can be earned. Titles in increasing level of difficulty are Novice Agility (NA), Open Agility (OA), Agility Excellent (AX), and Master Agility Excellent (MX).

Tracking

Yorkshire Terriers have a very keen sense of smell, and they love to use it. Yorkies excel at tracking. Find out if your pet enjoys using his natural tracking abilities. Hide little treats around the house or yard for him to find. Make the game more complicated by creating a trail of treats, laid one to several hours in advance of the search, and gradually increasing the distance between treats. At the end of the trail, have a surprise waiting, such as a favorite treat, or toy, or *you*!

Tracking competitions use an invisible trail of human scent, which the dog follows to locate a glove at the end of the course.

Rally

Rally is less formal than obedience, although the dog has to follow commands. Exercises include heeling, turning, weaving, obstacles, sit, down, come, and other maneuvers, in no set pattern. Handlers can direct and praise their dogs while they perform.

The American Kennel Club offers competitions to accommodate owners with disabilities and dogs with disabilities. Rally is a fun alternative to agility open to all.

Freestyle

In freestyle, you and your Yorkie "dance" together. You select the music and make up the choreography and then take your dog

through various moves and tricks in time to the music. He can weave around your legs, jump over your legs, turn in circles, heel, walk forward and backward, and do anything else you train him to do. The variety and originality is limitless and depends on you. Judges and spectators watch you and your nimble canine perform.

Flyball

Flyball is a fast relay race. Dogs that play flyball are keen competitors. To participate, your Yorkie must be able to run very fast, catch a ball, and leap over low hurdles. Flyball is a team sport. Each team has two dogs, and two teams compete at the same time. When each team releases the first dog on their team, the dogs run down different but parallel courses, over four hurdles, and toward a box with a spring-loaded platform. When the dogs trigger their respective platforms, a ball shoots out from the corresponding box. The dogs catch their balls and race back down the course, back over the four hurdles. The second dog on each team is released when the first dog returns. The first dog team to finish the race wins.

Frisbee

Yorkies love to play Frisbee, and they are good at it. Just be sure to buy a small, soft Frisbee that won't hurt your pet's mouth or break his tiny teeth.

PET-FACILITATED THERAPY

For those owners who love to do community service, pet-facilitated therapy is a wonderful activity. Your tiny terrier can make a

big difference in someone's life. Sharing your Yorkie's affection and your time with others is one of the kindest things you can do.

Yorkie therapy dogs help people in many ways by visiting nursing homes, assisted-living facilities, rehabilitation centers, schools, facilities for people with disabilities, and senior citizen centers. During these visits, therapy Yorkies can do a variety of things, including quiet cuddling, sitting on laps and being petted, and entertaining by performing tricks. Yorkies can make people laugh and share stories and memories. Just petting a Yorkie can replace anxiety, sadness, and loneliness with laughter, happiness, and comfort.

Therapy dogs must be very well mannered, obedient, and clean. They must have solid temperaments and cannot be aggressive or shy. They *must* have the right personality for the job and they *must* love what they do.

Pet-facilitated therapy is an emotional and rewarding community service. If you think you and your Yorkie would make a great therapy team, contact a therapy dog organization (see Information) to learn what is required and how your Yorkie can become certified.

GAMES

Yorkshire Terriers enjoy all kinds of games, from hide-and-seek, to fetch, to Frisbee. Yorkies are quick, agile, and coordinated.

There is no limit to the fun and surprises you will have with your Yorkshire Terrier. Beautiful, intelligent, energetic, bold, versatile, and full of fun, the Yorkshire Terrier is everything a dog should be—socialite, guardian, hunter, athlete, traveling companion, and devoted friend—and much, much more! It's no surprise that this quintessential canine is the most adored terrier in the world.

Yorkshire Terriers are intelligent and learn quickly, as long as they are having fun. So make training a fun game, with lots of praise.

Your Yorkie must understand that you are the boss. Keep in mind that young Yorkies are easily distracted. They also bore easily and tire quickly. So make training interesting by keeping sessions short, ending on a positive note, and always giving generous praise along with some tasty treats.

A basic puppy class, or dog training class, is a good way to begin obedience training. There are as many different training classes and techniques as there are dogs and trainers. Talk to other Yorkie owners and trainers and visit classes, so you can decide which class is best for you and your Yorkie.

Come

First teach your pet his name. Train your Yorkie in an area free of noise and distractions. Start by calling his name whenever you feed him. Use small tidbits, along with a lot of enthusiastic praise, as a reward throughout the day whenever you say his name and he responds by looking at you or coming to you. Soon, your Yorkie will come to you when called, purely for the attention and love you give him.

Sit

Use a table to teach your puppy to sit. Start by saying his name to get his attention. Then say, "*Sit.*" Use a happy but firm voice. Hold a tidbit of food above his nose. As his head goes up to follow the tidbit, his rear legs will bend so his hindquarters drop. Give him a treat. If he jumps up or stands up, don't reward him. In the beginning you may apply gentle pressure on the rump to show him how to sit. Give him a treat and lots of praise when he does. Always say his name first to get his attention. Then say "*Sit*" and give him a few seconds to respond.

Down

Use a table to teach the *down* command. Start from a sitting position, say his name, and say "*Down.*" At the same time, show him a food reward, near the table surface and below his nose. He will lower his head to eat it. Repeat the process and hold the treat slightly lower, just below the tabletop, so he must bend his elbows and lower his body to reach it. The *down* command takes time to learn, but you will use it often for grooming your Yorkie. As you teach your Yorkie, you may have to gently and briefly hold him in position so he understands the command, but *don't* force him into position.

Stay

Stay is an important command. It could save your Yorkie's life. To prevent injury, don't use the table for this command. Your Yorkie may try to jump off the table to follow you and be hurt. Start by placing your Yorkie in the sit position and say "*Stay*." Wait a few seconds, then say, "OK," and give a food reward and praise. The word *OK* lets him know he completed the task. Gradually extend the length of time he must sit.

Leash Training

When your Yorkie comes when called and follows you, you can begin leash training. Begin by attaching a light line, such as string or yarn, to his collar and let him drag it behind him and play with it. Let him follow you around with the string dangling. When he is used to the string, replace it with a light leash and walk with him. Begin by following your puppy wherever he goes. Do not pull on his neck.

Next, hold the leash and encourage your puppy to follow you a short distance. Don't drag or pull on him. If he walks with you, then stops, coax him back to you and give him a food reward. He will quickly learn that there is no resistance if he stays close to you. As soon as you resume walking, praise him and end the training session with more praise and a food reward. Do not allow your Yorkie to wear a collar with a leash attatched to it unless he is being supervised!

Information

Breed and Kennel Clubs

Yorkshire Terrier Club of America
www.theyorkshireterrierclubofamerica.org

American Kennel Club (AKC)
8051 Arco Corporate Drive, Suite 100
Raleigh, NC 27617-3390
(919) 233-9767
www.akc.org

Canadian Kennel Club
89 Skyway Avenue, Suite 100
Etibicoke, Ontario, Canada M9W6R4
(416) 675-5511
www.ckc.ca

United Kennel Club
100 East Kilgore Road
Kalamazoo, MI 49001
(616) 343-9020
www.ukcdogs.com

Association of Pet Dog Trainers
150 Executive Center Drive,
    Box 35
Greenville, SC 29615
(800) 738-3647
www.adpt.com

Therapy Dog Organizations

Delta Society Pet Partners Program
875 124th Avenue NE #101
Bellevue, WA 98005
(425) 679-5500
www.deltasociety.org

Therapy Dogs International
88 Bartley Road
Flanders, NJ 07836
(973) 252-9800
www.tdi-dog.org

Therapy Dogs Incorporated
1919 Morrie Avenue
Cheyenne, WY 82003
(877) 843-7364
www.therapydogs.com

Health-related Associations and Foundations

American Kennel Club
AKC Canine Health Foundation
P.O. Box 900061
Raleigh, NC 27675-9061
(888) 682-9696
www.akcchf.org

American Veterinary Medical Association
930 North Meacham Road
Schaumberg, IL 60173
(800) 248-2862
www.avma.org

Information on Household Poisons

www.epa.gov
www.cdc.gov

Lost Pet Registries

AKC Companion Recovery
5580 Centerview Drive, Suite 250
Raleigh, NC 27606-3394
(800) 252-7894
found@akc.org
www.akccar.org

AVID Identification Systems, Inc.
3185 Hamner Avenue
Norco, CA 92860
(800) 336-2843
www.avidid.com

Home Again Microchip Service
(888) HOME AGAIN
www.public.homeagain.com

Periodicals
AKC Gazettte
(800) 533-7323
www.akc.org/pubs

AKC Family Dog
(800) 533-7323
www.akc.org/pubs

Dog Fancy
www.dogchannel.com/dog-magazines

Dog World
www.dogchannel.com/dog-magazines

Books

Coile, D. Caroline. *Yorkshire Terriers (Barron's Dog Bibles)*. Hauppage, NY: Barron's Educational Series, Inc., 2009.

Coile, D. Caroline. *The Yorkshire Terrier Handbook*. Hauppauge, NY: Barron's Educational Series, Inc., 2013.

Haynes, Richard. *Living with a Yorkshire Terrier*. Hauppauge, NY: Barron's Educational Series, Inc., 2003.

Linzy, Jan. *Yorkshire Terrier Champions, 1984–2001*. Incline Village, NV: Camino Books, 2003.

Vanderlip, Sharon and Ludwig, Gert. *1000 Dog Names from A to Z*. Hauppauge, NY: Barron's Educational Series, 2005.

Important Note

This pet owner's manual tells the reader how to buy or adopt, and care for, a Yorkshire Terrier. The author and publisher consider it important to point out that the advice given in the book is meant primarily for normally developed dogs of excellent physical health and sound temperament.

Anyone who acquires a fully-grown dog should be aware that the animal has already formed its basic impressions of human beings. The new owner should watch the animal carefully, including its behavior toward humans, and, whenever possible, should meet the previous owner.

Caution is further advised in the association of children with dogs, in meeting with other dogs, and in exercising the dog without a leash.

Even well-behaved and carefully supervised dogs sometimes do damage to someone else's property or cause accidents. It is therefore in the owner's interest to be adequately insured against such eventualities, and we strongly urge all dog owners to purchase a liability policy that covers their dog.

Index

About the Author

Sharon Vanderlip, DVM, has provided veterinary care to domestic and exotic animal species for more than 35 years. She has authored more than 20 books on dog breeds and animal care and published numerous articles for scientific, veterinary, and general reading audiences.

Dr. Vanderlip served as clinical veterinarian for the University of California San Diego School of Medicine and has collaborated on reproductive research projects with the San Diego Zoo. She is former chief of veterinary medicine for the National Aeronautics and Space Administration (NASA) and former chief of surgery for a large national research institution specializing in reproductive medicine.

Dr. Vanderlip has lectured at kennel clubs and veterinary associations worldwide. She has received awards for her writing and her dedication to animal health and care. She may be contacted at *www.sharonvanderlip.com.*

Cover Photos

Fotolia: evegenesis: front cover (left); CallallooFred: front cover (middle)

Shutterstock: Lari Olga: front cover (top right); Africa Studio: front cover (bottom right); dien: back cover; Phase4Studios: inside front cover; Konstantin Gushcha: inside back cover

Photo Credits

Fotolia: Africa Studio: page 37; Antonio Gravante: page 45; CALLALLOO CANDCY: page 76; CallallooFred: pages 4, 28, 39, 40, 43, 47 (right), 58, 63, 68, 73, 74, 80, 82, 87; cynoclub: page 83; dionoanomalia: pages 5, 79, 90; Dogs: pages 30, 33, 34, 65, 67; Ermolaev Alexander: page 49; evegenesis: pages 10, 22, 35, 71; Gorilla: pages 51, 59; JLSnader: pages 20, 29; katamount: page 92; ksi: page 27; liliya kulianionak: page 17; Pavel Timofeev: pages 48, 53; Ulf: page 18

Shutterstock: Africa Studio: pages 16, 19; dien: pages 3, 8, 91; Ermolaev Alexander: page 50; f8grapher: pages 9, 85; Forewer: page 47 (left); HELL-FOTO: page 89; Konstantin Gushcha: pages 2, 6, 7, 12, 23, 25, 31; mholka: page 15; Nikolai Tsvetkov: pages 11, 26, 46, 55; Odnolko: page 44; olegius: page 14; otsphoto: pages 11, 13; Phase4Studios: pages 86, 88; Scorpp: pages 54, 56, 57, 93; tsik: page 81

Acknowledgments

I thank my husband, Jack Vanderlip, DVM, for his valuable help as an expert veterinary consultant and evaluator—and for taking care of our animals, our practice, and our home projects so that I could have time to revise this book.

A Note on Pronouns

Many dog lovers feel that the pronoun "it" is not appropriate when referring to a beloved pet. For this reason, Yorkshire Terriers are referred to as "he" or "she" throughout this book.

All inquiries should be addressed to:
Barron's Educational Series, Inc.
250 Wireless Boulevard
Hauppauge, NY 11788
www.barronseduc.com

Library of Congress Catalog No.: 2014043641

ISBN 978-1-4380-0505-8

Library of Congress Cataloging-in-Publication Data
Vanderlip, Sharon Lynn.
 Yorkshire terriers / Sharon L. Vanderlip, D.V.M. — 2nd edition.
     pages cm — (A complete pet owner's manual)
 Includes bibliographical references and index.
 ISBN 978-1-4380-0505-8
 1. Yorkshire terrier. I. Title.
 SF429.Y6V36 2015
 636.76—dc23   2014043641

Printed in China
9 8 7 6 5 4 3 2 1